The Open Court

Library of Philosophy

EUGENE FREEMAN, Editor
San Jose State College

ARISTOTLE
ON
HIS PREDECESSORS

ARISTOTLE
ON
HIS PREDECESSORS

Translated, with notes and introduction
by A. E. TAYLOR

FELLOW OF MERTON COLLEGE, OXFORD
FROTHINGHAM PROFESSOR OF PHILOSOPHY
McGILL UNIVERSITY, MONTREAL

With a new Foreword by
HERMAN SHAPIRO

PROFESSOR OF PHILOSOPHY
SAN JOSE STATE COLLEGE

OPEN COURT • ESTABLISHED 1887 • LA SALLE, ILLINOIS
Second Edition • 1969

ARISTOTLE
ON
HIS PREDECESSORS

Printed in the United States of America
By PAQUIN PRINTERS, Chicago

FOREWORD

I

All of the writings of the pre-Socratic philosophers have been lost. Such knowledge of pre-Socratic philosophy as we now possess derives from three main sources: the fragmentary "sayings" of the philosophers contained in the doxographical literature; the compilation of *Lives and Opinions of the Philosophers* which goes by the name of Diogenes Laertius; and the remarks made by Aristotle on his predecessors in Book I of the *Metaphysics*.

The history of philosophy composed by Aristotle's pupil, Theophrastus, provided the ancient world with its principal source of information concerning pre-Socratic thought. Unhappily, Theophrastus' original work appears to have been lost quite early, and is available to us today only in fragmentary form. Before its loss, however, Theophrastus' book served a great many antique authors as a basis for their own handbooks on the history of philosophy. These epitomizers and compilers of histories for whom Theophrastus' work served thus—either directly or indirectly—as a primary source, are known to modern scholarship as *doxographers*. It is their works which comprise the doxographical literature.

The two most important doxographical texts now available are the *Placita philosophorum* of the pseudo-Plutarch, compiled about 150 A.D.; and the doxographical extracts recorded in Book I of John Stobaeus' *Eclogae*, written about 470 A.D. Both of these works appear to have been drawn from the doxography of Aëtius—the so-called *Aëtii Placita*—composed about 100 A.D. Aëtius' work, in turn, employed as its chief source the *Vetusta Placita* compiled by an unknown disciple, or disciples, of the Stoic, Poseidonius, sometime during the first half of the first century A.D. This key work is lost to us: but that it did once exist; that it did serve as Aëtius' source; and that it was itself based upon the history of Theophrastus, has been shown by H. Diels in a brilliant work of scholarly detection.[1]

Sometime between 200 and 170 B.C., Sotion of Alexandria composed a work of philosophical biography titled *Successions of the Philosophers*. Although not wholly lacking in elements of doxographical interest, Sotion's book was mainly concerned to trace the historical development of the schools of philosophy flourishing in his day. According to Sotion, these schools grew out of two parallel lines of development: an *Ionic,* leading directly from Thales to the Middle Academy and Chrysippus; and an *Italic,* which led from Pythagoras to Epicurus by way of the Eleatics, Atomists, Sophists

[1] See Hermann Diels, *Doxographi Graeci* (Berlin: W. de Gruyter et Socios, 1879).

and Skeptics. In order, however, to establish the historical "successions" obtaining between these schools, Sotion was not infrequently forced to fabricate, quite arbitrarily, a master-disciple relation between earlier and later representatives of the different philosophical sects.

The *Successions* of Sotion, like Theophrastus' *History*, was soon to provide grist to the mills of the epitomizers and compilers of handbooks who flourished increasingly as the Hellenic spirit waned. A whole succession of *Successions* appeared: works, for the most part, in which the authors attempted to improve on Sotion's already dubious biographical material by the addition of apocryphal anecdotes and unauthentic apophthegms. Diogenes Laertius' *Lives and Opinions of the Philosophers,* composed in the early third century A.D., is the last representative of this genre, and the only one to come down to us in a fully-preserved state. Diogenes' book contains the residue of the whole literature of *Successions* developed in the centuries that lie between him and Sotion.

When A. E. Taylor notes, quite correctly, that the first book of Aristotle's *Metaphysics* constitutes, when *cautiously interpreted,* "the most valuable single document for the history of Greek philosophy,"[2] he goes far to define the actual state of our knowledge concerning the pre-Socratics. In this work, as well as other of his writings in which he remarks the notions of the early

[2] See below, p. 32.

Greek thinkers,[3] Aristotle is trying to establish his own views, not to furnish posterity with an objective historical account of his predecessors'. It is, indeed, extremely doubtful whether the philosophical problems which concerned him—problems which invariably provide the context within which he sets forth these prior doctrines—would have meant much to the men of whom he writes. Hence, Professor Taylor's entirely justified admonition to employ scholarly "caution" when examining Aristotle's testimony on the pre-Socratics.

As our knowledge of pre-Socratic philosophy can extend no further than our sources will permit, the present situation concerning that knowledge may be summed up thus: the doxographical fragments are invaluable—*but* they can be made to verify any theory of history or development that one happens to entertain by simply arranging and interpreting them in a suitable manner. The last generation of historians of ancient philosophy have almost uniformly succumbed to this temptation. To escape scholarly seduction the student is advised to read the fragments themselves before commencing any of the romances that have been built around them. Diogenes Laertius' testimony is similarly indispensable—*but* it is filled with conflicting and even contradictory accounts of the lives and opinions of the philosophers. Essentially, Diogenes' book is a late Roman, popular "Story of

---

[3] See, for example, Aristotle's *Physics,* Book I, and *De Anima,* Book I.

Philosophy," filled to the brim with old wives' tales and easily-remembered catchwords. Its chief importance, truth to tell, lies in its being the only ancient story of philosophy to come down to us in a complete state of preservation. Aristotle's remarks on his predecessors are "the most valuable" clues that we possess—*but,* as we have seen, even these bits must be "cautiously interpreted." If the student reads these three main sources of information and arrives at the conclusion that he knows far less about early Greek thought than the historians of philosophy, he will have progressed a good way on the road to Socratic wisdom.

II

Now directly we cease, as historians, to lament the shortcomings of Aristotle's presentation of early Greek thought, and begin to focus, as philosophers, on the question of just why he rehearses pre-Socratic doctrines in his writings at all, a wholly new approach to understanding the nature of Aristotle's remarks on his predecessors emerges. Viewed, indeed, from this perspective, all merely historical assessments concerning the value of Aristotle's testimony become totally irrelevant. The plain truth, as was previously stated, is that Aristotle

---

4 For examples of the newer, more fruitful way of treating the philosophy of the early Greek thinkers, see C.H. Kahn, *Anaximander and the Origins of Greek Cosmology* (New York: Columbia University Press, 1960); and P. Wheelwright, *Heraclitus* (Princeton, N.J.: Princeton University Press, 1959).

was never concerned to write philosophical history. Such historical value as his treatment of the pre-Socratics involves is thus merely accidental to his central concern; and that concern, as we have seen, was to establish his own philosophical views. A wholly proper question then, is: just how did Aristotle's remarks on his predecessors figure in this—his own—enterprise?

The Aristotelian method of inquiry, as we are given it to understand from a study of the procedures actually employed in his scientific writings, consists in five moments: first, precise delimitation of the subject-matter under investigation; second, a statement of previous "opinions" or hypotheses purporting to order the subject-matter in question; third, prosecution of a "dialectical" examination of these hypotheses; fourth, searching out of the facts relevant to the subject-matter under consideration; and fifth, exhibition of the subject-matter's factual content as intelligibly ordered in the light of the ultimately satisfactory hypothesis.[5] It is, then, steps two and three that bear directly upon the question at issue.

Step two gives a formalized expression to that profound sense of the continuity of inquiry which is so

[5] The best full treatment of Aristotle's methodology is still R. Eucken's, *Die Methode der aristotelischen Forschung in ihrem Zusammenhang mit den philosophischen Grundprinzipien des Aristoteles* (Berlin: Weidmannsche Buchandling, 1872). For a shorter, but no less excellent treatment of Aristotle's methodology, see Émile Boutroux, "Aristotle," in *Historical Studies in Philosophy* (London: Macmillan and Co., 1912).

characteristic a feature of the Aristotelian temper. Investigation in the arts and sciences, as Aristotle sees it, is a living, on-going process involving all searchers after truth, past and present. "In all discoveries," he writes in the *Sophistic Refutations,*

> either the results of other people's work have been taken over and after having been first elaborated have been subsequently advanced step by step by those who took them over, or else they are original inventions which usually make progress which at first is small but of much greater utility than the later development which results from them. . . . When, however, the first beginning has been discovered, it is easier to add to it and develop the rest. This has happened with rhetorical composition, and also with practically all the other arts. Those who discovered the beginnings of rhetoric carried them forward quite a little way, whereas the famous modern professors of the art, entering into the heritage, so to speak, of a long series of predecessors who had gradually advanced it, have brought it to its present perfection.[6]

And in a famous passage occurring in Book Alpha Minor of the *Metaphysics,* Aristotle again expresses his characteristic respect for the funded experience of the past—

[6] Aristotle, *Sophistic Refutations,* tr. E. S. Forster (Cambridge, Mass.: Loeb Classical Library, Harvard University Press, 1934), ch. xxxiv, 183b.

the real basis for his much-remarked "conservatism" and "traditionalism"—in this way:

> Whereas no one person can obtain an adequate grasp of Truth, we cannot *all* fail in the attempt; each thinker makes some statement about the natural world, and as an individual contributes little or nothing to the inquiry; but a combination of all conjectures results in something considerable. . . . It is only fair to be grateful not only to those whose views we can share but also to those who have expressed rather superficial opinions. They too have contributed something; by their preliminary work they have formed our mental experience.[7]

Hence, Aristotle will always take seriously the opinions of his Greek predecessors. Their views, to be sure, are not taken as final expressions of truth, but are accepted rather in precisely the way in which Aristotle accepts all features of his Greek heritage: as matter to be carefully worked over and artfully developed in order to actualize that which is best in it. And it is the actual process of reworking and developing that brings us, with Aristotle, directly to step three: the "dialectical" examination of the hypotheses made available by his predecessors.

Aristotle distinguishes three types of reasoning or

---

[7] Aristotle, *Metaphysics,* tr. H. Tredennick (Cambridge, Mass.: Loeb Classical Library, Harvard University Press, 1936), Book Alpha Minor, ch. i, 993b.

syllogism: dialectical; eristic; and scientific. The three types differ not at all in formal structure; the difference between them lies solely in the character of the premises from which they proceed. The scientific syllogism employs as premises those which are "primary and true" :[8] such, that is, which are the absolutely first, undemonstrable, principles of demonstration peculiar to the distinctive subject matters of the different sciences. The eristic syllogism, by contrast, concludes from premises which, far from being true, are "based on opinions which appear to be generally accepted, but are not really so" ;[9] while the dialectical syllogism employs as premises those views which "commend themselves . . . to all of the wise, or the majority, or to the most famous and distinguished of them."[10] To each of these three types of reasoning, Aristotle devotes a separate treatise of the *Organon*. The scientific syllogism is treated in the *Posterior Analytics;* the eristic, in the *Sophistical Refutations,* and the dialectical, in the *Topics.*[11] Clearly, the opinions set forth in accordance with step two of the Aristotelian procedure are such that admit of no treatment other than the dialectical. These views *are,* as we have seen, precisely

[8] Aristotle, *Topics,* tr. E. S. Forster (Cambridge, Mass.: Loeb Classical Library, Harvard University Press, 1935), Book I, ch. i, 100a.

[9] *Ibid.,* 100b.

[10] *Ibid.*

[11] For a clear and enlightening account of the development of Aristotle's logical thought, see E. Kapp, *Greek Foundations of Traditional Logic* (New York: Columbia University Press, 1942), ch. I.

those held by the "most famous and distinguished" of thinkers. Accordingly, if we wish to understand the procedures by means of which the views of his predecessors are to be reworked and developed, it is to the *Topics* that we must direct our attention.

In the *Topics,* Aristotle conceives of dialectic, broadly, as the science of what happens when men who entertain certain notions concerning the truth of things become involved in a discussion with the object of convincing one another. Thus conceived, dialectic is the reasoning of conversation; of Socratic dialogue; of the Sophists; of the whole Hellenic world of inspired talk and sustained political argument. In its more specific, scientific, application, however,[12] it is the function of dialectic to develop all the implications of any proposed principle of scientific explanation with an eye to revealing which are to be rejected because they lead to contradiction; or which are untenable because logically entailed consequences simply do not square with observed matters of fact. The scientific function of dialectical examination, in a word, by bringing to light all the difficulties and problems to which we are led by unsatisfactory hypotheses, at the same time discovers to us all the conditions and facts that the satisfactory hypothesis will have to meet and take into account. The formulation of adequate

---

[12] The uses of dialectic, Aristotle tells us, are three in number: (1) for mental training; (2) for general conversation; and (3) for application to the sciences. See *Topics, op. cit.,* Book I, ch. i.

hypotheses, as the third step of the Aristotelian procedure makes clear, is not accomplished by working with
the facts alone, but by working with the facts from
within the midst of a critical examination of all hypotheses available to account for them.

The answer to our question concerning the manner in
which Aristotle's remarks on his predecessors figured in
the establishment of his own philosophical views, is now
complete. For Aristotle, as we have seen, all scientific
demonstration depends upon certain ultimate premises
which are true and immediate. Since these first principles
of the sciences cannot themselves be scientifically demonstrated, the approach to them must be through the
dialectical examination of the opinions which "the wise"
have held about them. Not to begin from this point, as
Aristotle sees it, would be to give up the perspective on
truth afforded by "standing on the shoulders of giants."
Hence, we find that in the opening sections of any of his
scientific treatises—as in Book I of the *Metaphysics*—
Aristotle will subject the hypotheses advanced by his
predecessors to a piercing dialectical examination, modi-
fying and reformulating them until they are satisfactory
to serve as the principles of the subject-matter under
investigation.

Herman Shapiro

San Jose State College
January, 1969

SELECTED BIBLIOGRAPHY

I

PRIMARY SOURCES

Since Aristotle's philosophy is so intimately bound up with language and with problems of definition and classification, a good translation is almost impossible. A fairly satisfactory complete English translation is published in twelve volumes by the Oxford Press, under the general editorship of J. A. Smith and W. D. Ross; but the translations in the Loeb Classical Library edition of Aristotle's works are on the whole preferable. The best single volume edition of selections is: McKeon, R. (ed.) *The Basic Works of Aristotle.* New York: Random House, 1941.

II

SECONDARY SOURCES

Allan, D.J. *The Philosophy of Aristotle.* New York and London: Oxford University Press, 1952.

Anscombe, G.E.M. and Geach, P.T. "Aristotle" in *Three Philosophers.* Ithaca, New York: Cornell University Press, 1961.

Case, Thomas. "Aristotle." In *Encyclopedia Brittanica,* 11th ed.

Cherniss, H. *Aristotle's Criticism of Plato and the Academy*. Baltimore, Md.: Johns Hopkins University Press, 1944.

. . . . *Aristotle's Criticism of Presocratic Philosophy*. Baltimore, Md.: Johns Hopkins University Press, 1935.

Jaeger, Werner. *Aristotle: Fundamentals of the History of His Development*. New York and London: Oxford University Press, 1934.

Lukasiewicz, Jan. *Aristotle's Syllogistic*. New York and London: Oxford University Press, 1957.

Mure, G.R.G. *Aristotle*. London: Benn, 1932.

Randall, J. H. *Aristotle*. New York: Columbia University Press, 1960.

Ross, W.D. *Aristotle*. London: Methuen, 1930.

Santayana, George. "The Secret of Aristotle," in *Dialogues in Limbo*. New York: Scribners, 1926.

Shute, C.W. *The Psychology of Aristotle*. New York: Columbia University Press, 1941.

Solmsen, Friedrich. *Aristotle's System of the Physical World*. Ithaca, New York: Cornell University Press, 1960.

Spicer, E.E. *Aristotle's Conception of the Soul*. London: University of London Press, 1934.

Taylor, A.E. *Aristotle*. London: Nelson, 1943.

Wheelwright, P. *Aristotle*. New York: Odyssey Press, 1951.

CONTENTS

ARISTOTLE
ON
HIS PREDECESSORS

PREFACE.

PREFACE

PREFACE.

The present little work makes no ambitious pretence to originality of any kind. Its object is simply to supply students and teachers of philosophy, especially on the American continent, with a faithful rendering of Aristotle's critical sketch of the history of Greek speculative thought down to his own time. Having experienced the need of such a work in connection with my own lectures at McGill University, I have thought that others of my colleagues may also be glad that the want should be, in however imperfect a manner, remedied. This cannot, I think, be done by the reissue of any translation, however meritorious in itself, dating from a period in which our knowledge both of the text of Aristotle and of the early history of Greek thought was more imperfect than is at present the case. Accordingly, I submit to the judgment of my colleagues the accompanying new version, originally made for the purposes of my own lectures, trusting that they also may find it of some service. The translation has been based upon W. Christ's text of the *Metaphysics*, published in the Teubner series (2nd edition, Leipzig, 1903), and in the very few cases in which I have found it necessary to depart from that text in favor of readings of other critics

7

the fact has been carefully recorded in a foot-note. I have also, except where the contrary is specified, followed the guidance of Christ in the indication of glosses, which are marked in my translation, as in his text, by square brackets.

The brief notes which I have appended to the translalation do not in the least aim at providing anything like an editorial commentary. In general, their object is merely to supply either exact information as to the Greek terms represented by certain words in the translation, or to give references which appear indispensable to the comprehension of the author's meaning. Here and there in the pages which deal with the Platonic theory of Ideas I have, indeed, allowed myself to transgress these self-imposed limitations, and can only plead in excuse the abstract character of the topics treated of and the unfamiliar form of their presentation.

With regard to the style of the translation, I would only say that, while I have tried to reproduce as nearly as I can the effect upon my own mind of Aristotle's characteristic manner of exposition, and in particular to find some single stock translation for each technical expression of the Peripatetic system which occurs in our book, I have found it quite impossible to produce, in the rigid sense, a "wordfor-word" rendering. I have constantly been obliged, from the exigencies of readable English prose, to vary the English equivalents employed for certain Greek phrases and

words of ambiguous signification. I may note in particular that I have preferred "entity," which, in general, in
my version represents the Greek φύσις in its widest sense
of "determinate object of discourse," also to the more cus-
tomary "substance" as a translation of οὐσία in passages
where the term appears to be used broadly as an equivalent
for φύσις in the sense above explained, without reference
to its more special significance in Aristotle's own philosophy, viz., that which is a subject of predicates, but not
itself a predicate of any further subject. "Entities" I
have also employed occasionally, as the most non-committal
term I can find, to translate the substantive use of the Greek
neuter adjective with the definite article. αἴτιον and αἰτία,
again, which I commonly render by "cause," I have had
once or twice for reasons of language to translate "reason"
or "reason why." I have, however, striven to reduce the
possibility of misunderstanding by giving, wherever it
seemed necessary, the precise Greek original of any ambiguous term in the foot-notes. I ought also to remark that
I have, wherever possible, replaced the Greek prefix αὐτο,
when used with reference to the Platonic Ideas, by the
adjective "Ideal." Readers accustomed to the terminology of modern exact Logic will perhaps object to my em-
ployment of "exists," "existence" as synonyms with "is,"
"Being," as renderings of ἐστί, εἶναι, etc. This has, however, been done deliberately on the ground that the absence of distinction between existential and non-existen-

tial propositions is a fundamental characteristic of Aristotelian thought.

The works upon which I have most constantly depended in preparing the translation are naturally three: (1) The Greek commentary of Alexander of Aphrodisias on the *Metaphysics* (latest edition by Hayduck in the collection of *Commentaria in Aristotelem Græca*, published by the Berlin Academy). (2) Bonitz's edition of the text of the *Metaphysics* with Latin Commentary (Bonn, 1848). (3) Bonitz's posthumously published German translation of the *Metaphysics* (Berlin, 1890). To the last, in particular, I am frequently indebted for the first suggestion of appropriate renderings.

It only remains to express my obligation to Dr. Paul Carus for his ready response to my suggestion that this volume should be included in the *Philosophical Classics* of the *Religion of Science Library*.

MONTREAL, May, 1906.

INTRODUCTION.

INTRODUCTION.

I.

LIFE OF ARISTOTLE.

In or about 335 B. C. Aristotle of Stagira, a small city
of the Chalcidic peninsula, took up his permanent residence
in Athens as the head of a philosophical school, being at
the time a man of some forty-nine or fifty years. This
post he continued to fill until a few months before his death,
which took place some twelve or thirteen years later (332
B. C.). His early history, so far as it is relevant to the
understanding of his works, may be told in a few words.
He came of a family in which the medical profession was
herditary; his father, Nicomachus, held the post of court
physician to Amyntas II., King of Macedonia. It can scarcely
be doubted that these early associations with medicine
largely account for both Aristotle's wide acquaintance with
natural history, as evinced by a whole series of works on
zoology, and for the preponderatingly biological cast of
thought which is characteristic of his philosopy as a whole.
At the age of eighteen he had entered the philosophical
seminary of Plato, of which he continued to be a member

until Plato's death, twenty years later (346 B. C.).   Somewhat later (343-336 B. C.) he filled for several years the post of tutor to the Crown Prince Alexander of Macedonia, afterwards Alexander the Great.   On the accession of Alexander to the throne the ex-tutor withdrew, as already stated, to Athens and devoted himself to the organization of his scientific and philosophical school.   During the short period of Anti-Macedonian reaction which broke out in Athens upon the death of Alexander (323 B. C.), Aristotle, from his old connection with the Macedonian Court, naturally became an object of attack.   A prosecution for "impiety," i. e., disloyalty to the state religion, was set on foot, and, as there was no possible defense to be made, the philosopher anticipated the verdict by a voluntary exile, in which he died a few months later (322 B. C.).[1]

At the time when Aristotle opened his "school" in the Lyceum,[2] or gymnasium attached to the temple of Apollo Lyceus, there were already in existence two such institutions for the prosecution of the higher education, that of Isocrates, in which the instruction was mainly of a practical kind,

[1] The chief ancient authority for the life of Aristotle is the biography by Diogenes Laertius.   There are also one or two shorter anonymous "lives," which are commonly reprinted in complete editions of the "works," and a valuable summary, with dates, by Dionysius of Halicarnassus, the principal parts of which the student will find in R. P. 297.

[2] From the existence in this institution of a *Peripatos*, a covered portico for exercise in unfavorable weather, comes the name *Peripatetic* as a designation for the Aristotelian School.

designed as a preparation for public political and forensic life, and that of Plato, now presided over by Xenocrates, specially given up to metaphysical, ethical, and mathematical research. To these Aristotle added a third, which speedily distinguished itself by the range and variety of its investigations in what we should now call "positive" science, and especially in the biological, social, and historical sciences. These institutions resembled our "universities" in their permanent organization and the wide scope of their educational program, as well as in the adoption of the formal oral lecture and the "seminar," or informal discussion between master and students, as the principal methods of instruction. The chief differences between the ancient philosophical school and the modern university are, on the other hand, the absence from the former of any provision for the support of the master or "professor" by fees or systematic endowments, and the prolongation of the relation of master and pupil through a much longer period, often until the death of one or the other. The character of the philosophical writings of Aristotle (such as the *Metaphysics, Physics, Ethics*) makes it clear that they are for the most part not "works" prepared for circulation at all, but the manuscripts of a "professor's" lectures, written out in full for oral delivery, and preserved after his death by disciples whose main object was, not to construct readable and well-arranged books, but to preserve the maximum of the master's words at any cost in repetitions and *longueurs*.

It is only on this supposition that we can reasonably account for the inequalities, abruptness, and frequent irregularity of their style, and the extraordinary amount of repetition which occurs in them.[1] The actual "literary works" of Aristotle were the dialogues, intended not for study in a philosophical seminary, but for general circulation among the reading public of Athens. These dialogues, which were presumably in the main composed while their author was still a member of the Platonic Academy and before he had entered on his career as the head of an independent institution, were widely celebrated in antiquity for their literary grace, a quality by no means conspicuous in the Aristotelian writings now extant; portions of them have been suspected by modern scholars to have been incorporated in some of the more elegant and popular parts of the existing writings, and others are occasionally quoted by later authors, but as a whole they have perished. Thus we have to compare the extant books of Aristotle, in respect of their literary character, not so much with those of Plato, or Descartes, or Hume, as with the posthumously published volumes of lectures by which the philosophy of Hegel has chiefly been preserved.

[1] Cf. the remarks of Burnet, *The Ethics of Aristotle*, pp. **xi-xviii.**

II.

THE METAPHYSICS.

The fourteen books which contain the substance of Aristotle's lectures on the ultimate conceptions of philosophy
are cited by the ancient commentators and designated in
the MSS. by the title τὰ μετὰ τὰ φυσικά, whence has arisen
our name *Metaphysics*. The title, however, is one which
gives no indication of the nature of the subjects considered,
and is never employed by the author himself. τὰ μετὰ τὰ
φυσικά means, literally, simply the (lectures) which come
after the (lectures) on "Physics," and indicates only that
in the traditional arrangement adopted by ancient students
of Aristotle the fourteen books of *Metaphysics* were made
to follow on the eight books of φυσικά, or "Lectures on
Physics." This arrangement may have been adopted
either because, as the numerous allusions in the first
book of the *Metaphysics* to previous explanations given in
"our discourses on Physics" are enough of themselves to
show, Aristotle composed the *Metaphysics* after the *Physics*,
or because a knowledge of the main doctrines of the latter
is presupposed by the former, or for both reasons. (The
notion of some of the ancient expositors that the *Metaphysics* are so-called because the objects of which they treat are
more sublime and recondite than those of Physics is more
far-fetched and probably historically mistaken.)

When we ask what is the character of the subject which

Aristotle is expounding in these books, and how the science of "Metaphysics" differs from other sciences in scope and aim, we are thus thrown back from the insignificant title bestowed on the work by ancient tradition to a study of the names actually employed by Aristotle to denote this division of his philosophy. Of such names, we find, on inquiry, he has three. The subject of his present course of lectures is called "Wisdom," "Theology," "first Philosophy."[1] Of the three, the last is the most characteristic and, as we might say, the official designation of the science. Of the other two, "Wisdom" is simply an honorific appellative, indicative of Aristotle's conviction that "first Philosophy" is the highest and noblest exercise of the intellect; "Theology," again, is, so far as it goes, a correct designation, since "first Philosophy" is a study of ultimate first principles, and, in the Aristotelian Philosophy, God is such an ultimate principle. But God is only one ultimate principle among others, and thus "Theology," the doctrine of God, is, strictly speaking, only one part, though in a sense the culminating part, of the Aristotelian "first Philosophy."[2] What, then, is "first Philosophy," and what are the "second Philosophies" from which Aristotle wishes to discriminate it? To answer this question we have to turn our attention to Aristotle's classifi-

[1] For the name "wisdom" (σοφία), see chapters 1 and 2 of the present work, *passim*. For the other two designations, compare particularly the passage from *Metaphysics E*, 1, quoted below.

[2] Thus, strictly speaking, the "doctrine of God" only occupies half of one of the fourteen books of our existing *Metaphysics*, viz.: the second half of book *Λ* (c. s. 6-10).

cation of the sciences. The deepest and most radical distinction among the forms of knowledge, according to Aristotle, is that between the Theoretical or Speculative (θεωρητιxαί) and the Practical Sciences, a distinction roughly corresponding to that which we draw in English between the sciences and the arts. Speculative Philosophy (the *tout ensemble* of the speculative) differs from Practical Philosophy (the *tout ensemble* of the practical sciences) alike in its purpose, its subject-matter, and its formal logical character. The purpose of "theoretical" Philosophy as its name shows, is θεωρία, disinterested contemplation or recognition of truths which are what they are independently of our personal volition; its end is to *know*; the purpose of "practical" Philosophy, on the contrary, is to devise rules for successful interference with the course of events, to produce results which, but for our intervention, would not have come about; its end is thus to *do* or to *make* something. Hence arises a corresponding difference in the objects investigated by the two branches of Philosophy. Speculative Philosophy is exclusively concerned with what Aristotle calls τὰ μὴ ἐνδεχόμενα ἄλλως ἔχειν, "things which can by no possibility be otherwise," truths and relations independent of human volition for their existence, and calling merely for recognition on our part; "eternal verities," to speak after the fashion of Leibnitz. Practical Philosophy has to do exclusively with relations which human action can modify, things which can be altered in various ways; as Aristotle calls them, τὰ ἐνδεχόμενα ἄλλως ἔχειν, "things which can possibly be otherwise," the "contingent."

And hence arises again a logical difference between the conclusions of speculative and those of practical Science. Those of the former are rigidly universal truths which are deducible with logical necessity from self-evident axiomatic principles. Those of the latter, precisely because they relate to "what can possibly be otherwise," what is capable of alteration, are never rigid universals; they are *general* rules which hold good ὡς ἐπὶ τὸ πολύ, "in the great majority of cases," but which are all liable to occasional exceptions, owing to the unstable and contingent character of the facts with which they deal. It is, according to Aristotle, a convincing proof of a philosopher's ἀπαιδευσία, "lack of grounding in Logic," that he looks to the results of practical sciences (e. g., the detailed precepts of Ethics) for a higher degree of certainty and universality than the contingent nature of their subject-matter permits.[2]

[1] Cf. for all this, *Ethica Nicomachea* vi 2, 1139a 6-31, vi 4, 1140a 1-23

[2] Cf. e. g. *Ethica Nic.* I 3, 1094b 19. "Such being the nature of our subject-matter and our axiomatic principles, we must be satisfied with establishing results which are true roughly and in their general outline, and, since the facts of which we treat and the principles from which we reason are true only in the generality of cases, we must be content with conclusions of the same kind. . . . The man of logical training will only seek such a degree of certainty in each branch of study as the character of the objects studied permits. To demand demonstration from a statesman is an error of the same kind as to be content with probable reasoning in a mathematician."

"First Philosophy," then, is essentially a "speculative science;" its aim is *knowledge*, the *recognition* of eternally valid *truths;* not *action*, the production of changes in the contingent world-order around us. It is on this ground especially that in our present book Aristotle, with his characteristic preference for the life of the student rather than that of the "man of affairs," claims the honorific title of "wisdom," traditionally consecrated to the worthiest and most exalted form of mental activity, for "first Philosophy." We have next to determine the exact position of "first Philosophy" among the various divisions of "speculative science," and its relation to the sister branches. Plato, indeed, had taught that all the sciences are, in the end, deductions from a single set of ultimate principles which it is the business of the supreme science of "Dialectic" to discover and formulate.[1] On such a view there would, of course, be no "sister" branches, no "*second* Philosophy." Dialectic would, in the last resort, be not only the supreme but the *only* science, just as a growing school of thinkers maintains to-day that all "exact" or "pure" science is simply Logic. This is, however, not Aristotle's view. According to him, speculative philosophy falls into a number of distinct and independent, though not co-ordinate, branches, each with its own characteristic special subject of investigation, and its own special axiomatic principles. "First Philosophy," though, as we shall see directly, the

[1] Plato, *Republic* vi, 510b-511d.

paramount branch of speculative science, is only *prima inter pares*.

How many distinct branches of speculative science, then, are there? Aristotle answers that there are *three*, "first" Philosophy, Mathematics, Physics. The logical basis of this classification is explained in the following important passage from *Metaphysics E*, 1, 1026a 10-32: "If there is anything which is eternal and immutable and has an independent and separable existence,[1] manifestly the cognition of it belongs to speculative science, since it is neither the object of Physics (which is a science of things capable of motion) nor of Mathematics, but of a study logically prior to both of them." For Physics deals with objects which have no existence separable [from matter, TR.], but are not devoid of motion, and Mathematics, in some of its branches,[2] with objects which are incapable of motion and have, perhaps, no separable existence, but are inherent in matter, whereas the objects of first Philosophy are both separate and devoid of motion.

[1] "Independent and separable;" Greek, χωριστόν. The double epithet seems required in English to bring out the full sense.

[2] The qualification is inserted simply because Aristotle has not yet given the formal proof, that the objects of Geometry and Arithmetic themselves are not independent entities, but mere predicates of matter, though investigated by the mathematician in abstraction from the matter which, in fact, they qualify. This proof he attempts later in *M*. 3. At present, he seems to be merely appealing to the existence of such branches of mathematics as Optics and Harmonics as obvious examples of the distinction in question.

Now, all causes must necessarily be eternal, but most of all these, for they are the causes of the visible divine things.[1] Thus there will be three speculative philosophies, the mathematical, the physical, the theological. For, manifestly, if the divine exists at all, it is to be found in such a class of entities as that just described, and the noblest science must have the noblest class of objects for its study. Thus the speculative sciences are of superior worth to all others, and this study of superior worth to the rest of the speculative sciences.

The question might, indeed, be raised whether first philosophy is of universal scope or confined to the study of a single department and a single class of entities. For even in Mathematics, the different branches are not co-ordinate; Geometry and Astronomy are confined to special classes of entities, but universal Mathematics[2] embraces all alike. If, then, there are no substances besides those which arise in the course of nature, Physics will be "first" Philosophy. But if there is a substance which is immutable, it will be logically prior, and the Philosophy which studies it will be "first" Philosophy, and because "first" will be universal. And it will be for this science to study Being as such, both as to what its funda-

[1] i. e., The heavenly bodies.

[2] i. e., Arithmetic, the principles of which are presupposed by every form of special mathematical study. Cf. below in the present book, C. 2, 982a 26.

mental character is and as to the attributes which are predicable of it *qua* Being.[1]

We see from this explanation both why there are three distinct branches of Speculative Science, and why one of the three has a logical position of priority over the other two, which justifies the name "first" Philosophy. "First" Philosophy, to begin with, is logically prior to the other sciences on the same ground on which Aristotle tells us in the present book that Arithmetic is "prior" to Geometry; its initial assumptions are simpler and less complicated than theirs. Physics is a study of the relations between objects which possess the double qualification of being embodied in concrete material form and being, potentially at least, in motion. In Mathematics one of these restrictions is removed; we consider objects (points, lines, surfaces) which are motionless and immutable, and the presuppositions of Mathematics are consequently so far simpler than those of Physics. (It was on this ground, it will be remembered, that Plato, in the educational scheme of Book vii. of the *Republic*, had contended that the study of Arithmetic and Geometry, plane and solid, should precede that of Kinetics or Astronomy.) But the other restriction

---

[1] Thus we get the following classification:

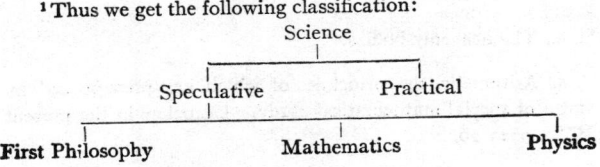

still remains. The objects of Mathematics, according to Aristotle, are still things which have no existence except as modifications or attributes of concrete material things. They are, in fact, the numerical properties of collections of concrete objects, or again, ideal boundaries and limits of sensible bodies. It is true that the mathematician makes abstraction from this fact, and treats it as though it were not there. He talks of numbers, lines, planes, etc., as though they were things with an independent existence of their own. But the fact, according to Aristotle, is none the less there, and it is the business of a sound Logic of the sciences to call attention to it. Numbers are really always numbers of something, of men, of horses, oxen, etc. "Two and two are four" means "two *men* (*horses*) and two *men* (*horses*) are four *men* (*horses*)." Only, as the numerical result is always the same whether you are counting men or horses, there is no need to specify the particular character of the objects you are counting. So with Geometry; a plane is, e. g., always the boundary of a certain physical solid body, only, for the purposes of Plane Geometry, it may not be necessary to take this into consideration.[1] But in "first" Philosophy this restriction, too, is removed. We study Being not, like the physicist, in so far as it is composed of

---

[1] I need not say that I am not here giving my adhesion to this view of the nature of mathematical science, but merely epitomising the position assumed by Aristotle.

bodies in motion,[1] or like the mathematician, in so far as it possesses number and spatial form, but in all its generality; we investigate what it means to *be*, and what relations between Beings are deducible from the great fundamental condition that they one and all *are*. This is why "first" Philosophy, as compared with the other speculative sciences, has a higher degree of universality in its scope. The propositions of the physicist become false if they are asserted about anything except bodies in motion; those of the mathematician become false when asserted of subjects which are neither numerable collections nor the spatial forms of bodies. The general principles of "first" Philosophy are applicable alike to God, to a geometrical figure, to a physical corpuscle, since each of these three is something of which you can say that it has *being* or *is*. At the same time, there is one class of "things which are" which may be regarded as constituting in a very special sense the object of "first" Philosophy, conversant though that science is, in a way, with everything. This is the class of immutable entities which have neither bodies nor spatial form of any kind, and are therefore excluded from the purview both of Physics and of Mathematics. The chief of such entities is God,

---

[1] Strictly speaking, this description unduly narrows the scope of Physics as conceived by Aristotle. With him "matter," the substratum of change, is not necessarily corporeal, and "motion" includes every species of quantitative and qualitative change. Thus, since the human soul is something which *grows* and *develops*, Psychology is a branch of Physics.

the immaterial and immutable source of the vital movement in the universe, and hence the appropriateness of the
name "Theology" or "Science of God" as a synonym for
"first Philosophy" itself. Now, Aristotle holds that any
complete explanation of any process, e. g., the simplest process of physical change, involves the introduction of this
concept of God as an eternal and immaterial "first mover;"
hence, the "doctrine of God" is the necessary crown and
culmination of the physical sciences themselves. This
explains how, in his conception of "first" Philosophy, the
notion of a "Science of God" and that of a most universal
science of the "principles of Being as such" come to be
so completely fused. The business of "first" Philosophy
thus comes to consist in the analysis of the conception of
individual Being or Substance (οὐσία) as such, i. e., the
determination of the fundamental meaning, the τί εστί
(or what is it?) of Being, and the analysis of individual Being
into its logical factors or elements. These constituent
factors constitute, in Aristotelian language, the *Causes* or
First Principles of Being. Thus it becomes possible to
describe the science of "first" Philosophy, as is done in the
opening chapter of our present book, as the Science of the
Causes and Principles of all Being. Aristotle believed himself to have finally performed the requisite analysis by his
doctrine of the Four Causes (see appendix B and the
notes there), and the part which they play in the development of the individual substance from mere possibility or

potentiality into actual existence. Accordingly, we find that the central books of our *Metaphysics* constitute a treatise of which the principal topics are the nature of individual substance, the doctrine of the four Causes, and the conception of the development from potential to actual existence. Outside this general scheme fall the two concluding books, *M* and *N*, which contain a polemic against the mathematical philosophy of the Pythagoreans and Plato; book *K*, a patchwork résumé, presumably by a later hand, of various portions of the *Physics* and *Metaphysics*; book *Δ*, a treatise on the principal equivocal terms of philosophy; book *a*, a brief introductory account of "first" Philosophy, which was widely recognized, even in antiquity, as non-Aristotelian; and our present book *A*, which forms an historical introduction to the whole work, and has the interest of being the earliest known systematic attempt at writing the History of Philosophy. As the present work is offered merely as a translation of this historical sketch, and not as a specimen of Aristotelian metaphysics, I shall at once proceed to terminate these introductory remarks with a few observations upon Aristotle's method of writing philosophical history.

III.

HISTORICAL VALUE OF ARISTOTLE'S CRITICISM.

Perhaps the greatest of the many obligations which human thought owes to Aristotle and his school is that they were the first thinkers to realize at all adequately the importance of systematic historical research into the evolution of ideas and institutions. To such research Aristotle would naturally be led both by his natural bias in favor of acquaintance with detailed scientific fact and by his early medical and biological training, which predisposes him to make the development of a finished and articulate product from crude and indeterminate beginnings the central conception of his whole philosophy. Accordingly, we find that the first systematic histories, alike of ideas and of social institutions, are all the work of Aristotle and his immediate pupils. Thus, to take only a few examples constitutional history, if we except a few tentative contributions from Plato,[1] begins with the series of sketches of political institutions in various commonwealths, known to the ancients as the πολιτεία of Aristotle, though they

[1] See, particularly, the long and interesting passages on the successive transformations by which "patriarchal" government, according to Plato, passed into historical monarchy, and on the development of the Persian and Athenian constitutions in *Laws*, Book III. The better known sketch of the successive degenerations from the ideal constitution in *Republic*, Books VIII–IX, stands on a rather different footing, as its object is to establish an order of spiritual affinity rather than one of historical sequence.

must have been the work not of the master alone but of
a whole band of pupils, of which we have an extant specimen
in the recently recovered *"Constitution of Athens."* The
earliest sketches of the history of Philosophy and Psychology
are those contained in the present book and in the first book
of the treatise *de Anima*, respectively. The earliest outline
of the history of Physics is similarly that given by Aristotle
in the opening chapters of the first book of his *"Lectures on
Physics."* The first separate and complete history of Physics was composed by Aristotle's pupil and immediate suc-
cessor, Theophrastus, and the first history of Mathematics by
another disciple, Eudemus,[1] and it is principally to
second or third hand epitomes and to later citations from
these works that we are still indebted for our detailed
knowledge of the development of early Greek science in both
these departments.

To make a discriminating use of Aristotle's sketch of previous philosophical thought we need, however, to bear carefully in mind both the special object for which it is avowedly
designed, and certain mental peculiarities of its author. Our
present book, as Aristotle is careful to indicate, is meant

---

[1] The dependence of the epitome of physical theories known as
the *Placita Philosophorum*, which has been preserved to us in a double
form in the writings ascribed to Plutarch and in the *Eclogæ* of
Stobæus, on the lost *Φυσικαὶ Δόξαι* of Theophrastus was established by Diels in the prolegomena to his *Doxographi Græci*; the work
of Eudemus is mainly known to us from the use made of it by the Neo-
Platonic philosopher, Proclus, in his commentary on the first book of
Euclid's *Elements*.

not as an independent contribution to the history of thought, but strictly as an introduction to Aristotelian "first" Philosophy as expounded in the subsequent lectures. Its purpose is not to give a full account of the "systems" of previous thinkers, but to afford presumption that the Aristotelian classification of causes and principles is complete, by showing that it provides a place for every sense of "Cause," and every principle of explanation occurring in the works of the pre-Aristotelian philosophers. This anxiety to confirm his own views by pointing to partial anticipations of them by earlier thinkers, and even by popular unphilosophic opinion, is very characteristic of Aristotle, who was profoundly convinced, as he says himself in the *Ethics*,[1] that "a widely-held conviction must have *something* in it," and by no means shared Plato's superb disdain for conventional current "opinion" in matters of philosophy. No great philosopher has ever been farther removed than Aristotle from the mental attitude of a recent writer who protests eloquently against the intrusion into philosophy of " the vulgar prejudices of common sense." [2]

We have further to remember that Aristotle, like Hegel in later days, was convinced that his own philosophy was the "absolute" philosophy, the final formulation of that answer

---

[1] *Ethica Nic.*, 1173a1. "What *everybody* thinks to be good, that we say *is* good; he who rejects this ground of belief will not easily produce a more convincing one." Contrast Shelley's characteristic remark that "Everybody saying a thing doesn't make it true."

[2] Russell, *Principles of Mathematics*, I., 348.

to the problems of the human intellect which all previous thought had been vainly trying to express. Hence he looks upon all earlier systems, from the point of view of his own doctrine, as imperfect and "stammering" attempts to formulate a thought identical with his own. What he says more than once of Empedocles and Anaxagoras he might equally, from his own point of view, have said of all his predecessors: "If the consequences of their doctrines could have been put before them, they would have arrived at my own results; but there was no one to point out these consequences to them, and consequently they failed to make their theories consistent." Unlike Plato, Aristotle shows little of the imaginative sympathy which is required of any thinker who attempts to give an uncolored version of the thoughts of minds less informed and less developed than his own. Hence, if we relied upon the letter of his statements about cruder and older philosophies, we should often be led seriously astray; when we have, however, made allowance, as it is usually easy to do, for this tendency to read his own system into the utterances of his predecessors, what he tells us is, in general, of the highest importance, and it is hardly too much to say that the first book of the *Metaphysics*, thus cautiously interpreted, is by far the most valuable single document for the history of early Greek Philosophy.[1]

Aristotle's version of the development of previous Greek philosophical thought may be briefly summarised as follows.

[1] See Burnet, *Early Greek Philosophy*, p. 370, on which these remarks are largely founded.

The earliest thinkers unconsciously adopted the standpoint of a materialistic Monism. They assumed that the only things which exist are the physical bodies perceived by our senses, and that the only question which science has to ask about them is, what is the one ultimate form of body of which they are all transformations? (The Milesian school, Heraclitus.) In Aristotelian language, they were interested only in the *material* cause of bodies, the *stuff* of which they are made, and they assumed that there is ultimately only one such original stuff and that it is one of the perceptible forms of matter.[1] Their later successors (Empedocles, Anaxagoras, the Atomists) saw that from such a point of view it is more plausible to regard sensible bodies as complexes of many different and equally primary constituents, and thus materialistic Monism gave way to Pluralism on the question of the material cause. At the same time, half unconsciously, they felt the need of asking a second question: What provides the motive impulse by which these constituents have been brought into just these combinations, and no others? Thus we get a first confused recognition of the existence of *efficient* causes and their indispensability to complete scientific explanation. (Empedocles, Anaxagoras.) As order, arrangement, organization are naturally recognized as good, and their opposites as evil, this entails further the notion of a *final* cause or rational purpose as present in the order of nature, and thus the conception of *end* or *purpose* makes its appear-

[1] The last clause is scarcely applicable to Anaximander, whom Aristotle ignores as completely as he can throughout this sketch.

ance, though at first in a form in which the final and efficient causes of the natural order are not properly discriminated. (Empedocles, Anaxagoras.) Meanwhile, attention had been directed in an unsystematic way by the Pythagorean mathematicians to the importance of discovering the *law* or constitutive formula by which the elementary constituents of each different kind of object are combined. Socrates further developed this interest in *formal causes* or constitutive formulæ by his insistence on the importance for Ethics of accurate *definitions* of the various virtues. From these initial impulses arose the Ideal Theory of Plato, in which the conception of the formative law or *formal cause*, as hypostatised into a transcendent noumenon, is made the center of a great philosophical system, to the neglect, as Aristotle thinks, of the equally important concepts of efficient and final cause. Thus the upshot of the whole review of philosophical history is, that all the four senses of causation discriminated in the *Physics* have received recognition by preceding thinkers, but that they have not yet been defined with sufficient accuracy or distinguished sharply enough from each other. The task thus indicated as essential to the thorough scientific explanation of things is the task that the Aristotelian "first" Philosophy undertakes to accomplish. It is plain that, though Aristotle does not say this in so many words, he regards as the specially important figures among his predecessors Anaxagoras and Plato; Anaxagoras, because by his doctrine of Mind as the formative cause of the world-order he first gave expression, in however inadequate and unconscious a way, to the teleological interpretation of the universe, and Plato, because he was the first philosopher to put the problem of determining the "forms" or "real essences" of the different kinds of objects in the forefront of philosophical inquiry.

The extent to which lack of sympathetic imagination has vitiated the historical character of Aristotle's sketch of preceding philosophy appears to vary considerably as we consider his treatment of the different schools. From the point of view of the most recent investigation, little can be objected against his treatment of the early Ionian Monists, from Thales to Heraclitus, except a tendency to employ in stating their views technical terms of his own system, such as ἀρχή, "principle," στοιχεῖον, "element," and the like. When allowance has been made for this habit, we readily see that Aristotle's interpretation of these naïve Monistic thinkers is in all essentials thoroughly historical. The same is true of his brief but lucid account of the Atomism in which pre-Sophistic physical science culminated, and his still briefer characterisation of the place of Socrates in the development of thought. We can hardly say as much for his treatment, in the present work, of Empedocles and Anaxagoras. The attempt to distinguish in the system of Empedocles between the "four elements" as the *material* and Love and Strife as the *efficient* causes of Nature is quite unhistorical, and Aristotle's own remarks on Empedocles in other writings show that he is fully aware of this. Similarly it is, from the point of view of objective historical fact, a misapprehension to censure Anaxagoras for his mechanical conception of the relation between Mind and the "mixture." The teleological significance read by Plato and Aristotle into the notion of Mind as the source of cosmic order was certainly not prominent, if present at all, in the actual thought of Anaxagoras. Still, it may possibly be said that Aristotle is avowedly undertaking rather to show how far the utterances of the earlier thinkers would permit of logical development into something like his own doctrine than to determine their actual original meaning. This defence has, no doubt, considerable weight, but one may be allowed to question whether it justifies the interpretation of Anaxagoras' "mixture" into a quasi-Aristotelian theory of "indeterminate matter," or the criticism of it in the light of the Aristotelian conception of chemical combination.

There remain three schools of thought towards which it seems impossible to deny, when all allowances for a philosopher's natural bias have been made, Aristotle shows himself unsympathetic and unjust, viz., the Eleatics, the Pythagoreans, the Platonists. The sources of his lack of sympathy are in all three cases fortunately easily discoverable. A biologically-minded philosopher to whom the development of the individual is the most salient fact of existence can hardly be expected to show much tenderness for thinkers who regard all change as mere illusion, and consequently, as Aristotle observes, leave no room for a science of Physics at all. Hence it is not strange that, though Aristotle elsewhere correctly indicates the important influence of Eleatic dialectic on the development of physical speculation,[1] his brief and unsympathetic observations in the present book should entirely obscure the fact that the criticism of Parmenides, by annihilating the logical basis of materialistic Monism, was really the most important turning-point in the whole history of pre-sophistic speculation.[2] It is unfortunate, also, that his account of the two great thinkers of the Eleatic school, Parmenides and Melissus, has been gravely vitiated in the case of Parmenides by the assumption that the dualistic cosmology of the second part of his poem represents the author's own views,[3] and in the case of Melissus, by a pedantic objection to that great thinker's incidental transgressions of the laws of formal logic.[4]

Similarly Aristotle's unsympathetic account of Pythagoreanism and Platonism is largely explained by the simple consideration that the leading ideas of both those philosophies are essentially mathematical, whereas Aristotle was by training and natural bent a biologist, and of a thoroughly non-mathematical cast of mind. His criticism of the mathematical philosophers in books *A, M, N* of the *Metaphysics* betrays much the same kind of misunderstanding as we should expect if a thinker of the antecedents of Herbert Spencer were to set himself to demolish the ideas, for instance, of

---

[1] *De Generatione,* A8.324b35 ff. (R. P. 148 A.) Compare Burnet, *op. cit.* 354-6.

[2] See Burnet, *op. cit.* p. 192.

[3] Cf. Burnet, *op. cit.* p. 195 ff.

[4] Burnet, *op. cit.* p. 341-2.

Weierstrass or Cantor.   In the case of the Pythagoreans, the difficulty of entering sympathetically into their thought was no doubt increased for Aristotle both by the naïveté with which their ideas were formulated, and by the absence of really trustworthy sources of information.   It is pretty clear that down to the time of Aristotle there was no Pythagorean literature in existence, and in its absence Aristotle would necessarily depend for information upon the verbal statements of such associates as the musician, Aristoxenus, whose historical good faith is far from being above suspicion.   (It is probably from the oral assertions of such associates who had been personally acquainted with the latest generations of Pythagoreans that Aristotle derived his decidedly improbable view that the Platonic doctrine of the "participation" of things in Ideas had been anticipated by Pythagoreanism.)[1] Whether we ascribe the result primarily to defective information or to mathematical incompetence, one thing at least is certain, viz., that chapters 5 and 8 of our present book are quite inadequate as an account of the thinkers who laid the foundations of scientific arithmetic and geometry, and made a nearer approximation to the true theory of the solar system than any other pre-Copernican men of science.   It is quite impossible to do justice to Pythagorean science, or even to understand its true character, unless the wretchedly inadequate discussion of Aristotle is supplemented by some

---

[1] See Burnet, *op. cit.* p. 302 ff, whose opinion as to the spuriousness of all the so-called fragments of "Philolaus," though not universally accepted by scholars, seems to me more than probable

historical account in which due prominence is given to the work of the school in Astronomy, Harmony, and pure Mathematics.[1] Aristotle, it should be noted, had composed a separate monograph on Pythagoreanism which is now lost, but can hardly, from his lack of sympathy with mathematical modes of thought, have possessed any high philosophical value.

The Aristotelian criticism of Platonism has given rise to a host of divergent opinions and a mass of the most tedious of human writings. Every possible view has been taken of it, from that of those who regard it as a crushing refutation of the vagaries of a transcendentalist dreamer of genius to that of those who refuse to believe that Plato can ever have taught anything so crazy as the doctrine Aristotle puts into his mouth. This is not the place to discuss at length topics on which I may have a more suitable opportunity of enlarging in the near future, and I will therefore merely record here one or two conclusions which seem to me to follow from any unbiased consideration of the anti-Platonic polemic of the *Metaphysics*.

Aristotle, lecturing during the life-time of Xenocrates,

---

[1] For excellent accounts of the school, see Bäumker, *Das Problem der Materie in der Griechischen Philosophie*, pp. 33-46; Milhaud, *Philosophes-Geomètres de la Grèce*, pp. 79-123; M. Cantor, *Geschichte der Mathematik*, I., pp. 137-175. It was the non-existence of written Pythagorean literature which gave rise in later ages to the fiction of the "Pythagorean Silence," the imaginary division of the order into an inner and outer circle, and the tale of the drowning of Hippasus in revenge for his publication of the secrets of the school. See Burnet, *op. cit.* p. 101 ff.

his fellow-pupil in the Platonic Academy, undoubtedly intended to give a *bona fide* account of the Platonic doctrine. A mere polemical misrepresentation, where the circumstances were such as to make exposure inevitable, would have been suicidal. It is also clear that Aristotle intends to present the doctrine in question as that of Plato himself, and not merely of Xenocrates and the contemporary Academy. This is shown by the occurrence of occasional direct references to expressions employed by Plato in his oral teaching, as well as by passages in which the views of particular contemporary Platonists are distinguished from those of "the first" author of the doctrine," i. e., Plato. Hence it seems to me indubitable that, although the doctrine of the Ideal Numbers and their derivation from the One and the "Great and Small" is not to be found *totidem verbis* in the Platonic dialogues, Plato must actually have said substantially what Aristotle makes him say on these topics. If a philosopher of the genius of Aristotle, writing after twenty years of personal association with a teacher of whose lectures he had himself been an associate editor, and in circumstances which make intentional misrepresentation incredible, cannot be trusted to give a substantially correct account of what his master said, surely there is an end to all confidence in human testimony. I would further suggest that the doctrine ascribed to Plato by Aristotle is in the main consistent and intelligible, and can be shown to be a natural development of positions which are actually taken up in several of the dialogues, notably the *Parmenides* and *Philebus*.

Most of the difficulties found in it by scholars have, I believe, been due to their own unfortunate unfamiliarity with the concepts of Mathematics and exact Logic. At the same time, I think it probable that Plato himself fell into occasional inconsistencies in the first formulation of such highly abstract principles, and certain that Aristotle, from lack of mathematical competence, has often failed to understand the meaning of the propositions he attacks. Some cases of such failure I have tried to indicate in my notes to chapter 9 of the present work. I will here terminate these introductory remarks with the two suggestions (1) that the growing interest of contemporary philosophers in the logic of the exact sciences promises to put us in a better position for comprehending the central thought of the Platonic theory than has ever been possible since its first enunciation,[1] and (2) that it would be an interesting subject for inquiry whether the forcing of all philosophic thought into biological categories by the genius of Aristotle has not fatally retarded the development of correct views on the logic of exact science right down to the present day.

[1] Particularly valuable as illustrating the light thrown on Plato's philosophy by a study of the mathematical problems in which it originated, is the work of Prof. G. Milhaud, *Les Philosophes-Géomètres de la Grèce*, to which I have several times had occasion to refer in the course of this book.

SUMMARY.

SUMMARY.

CHAPTER I.

Intellectual curiosity a fundamental natural instinct, as is shown by the fact that sense-perceptions are normally pleasant in themselves. The successive stages in the development of rational cognition: sensation, primary memory, experience, art or science [i. e., bodies of general truths which involve a theory as to the *reason* of facts and a systematic classification of them]. General theory, though often less serviceable for immediate practice than experience, holds a higher rank in the series of intellectual activities, because it involves insight into the *cause* or *reason* of facts; hence, we regard it as revealing a superior degree of *Wisdom*. Historically, human intelligence was first employed in providing for the necessities, and then for the comforts, of existence; science arose, in Egypt, from the existence of a priestly caste for whose necessities and comforts adequate provision had already been made, and who therefore were at leisure to employ their intellect upon speculative inquiry into the reasons and causes of things.

45

CHAPTER II.

What is the general character of that highest form of intellectual activity which is traditionally known as "Wisdom?" By universal consent, Wisdom possesses the following characteristics: (1) universality of range (conversance with the universal presuppositions of all cognition); (2) profundity; (3) ultimate certainty and validity; (4) finality in its explanations; (5) scientific disinterestedness; (6) independence of immediate practical needs. All these characteristics will be found to belong in a superlative degree to the scientific investigation of the ultimate causes and principles of existence. The original incentive to such investigation is the sense of wonder and perplexity in the presence of facts which we are unable to explain. The science thus originated, because independent of all practical interests, is the only really *liberal* science. It also, more than any other form of knowledge, is "divine," for the double reason that it involves the contemplation of divine objects and that it is the only form of cognition worthy of divine intelligences.

CHAPTER III.

Our object, then, is the analysis and classification of the different kinds of *cause*. In the *Physics* we have distinguished four senses of the term: (1) the *formal*, (2) the *material*, (3) the *efficient*, (4) the *final* cause. A review of the past history of philosophical thought will confirm our confidence in the exhaustiveness of this analysis if we find that every principle of explanation employed by previous thinkers can be classed under one or other of these four heads.

Now, the earliest philosophers asked only: What is the *material* cause of things—i. e., what is the primitive and indestructible body of which all sensible things are perishable transformations ? Thales, whose reasons for his opinion can only be conjectured, said that it is *water* (a view which perhaps has some support in early poetical tradition); Anaximenes and Diogenes, that it is *air;* Heraclitus and Hippasus, that it is *fire;* while Empedocles assumes the existence of four such primitive forms of body; Anaxagoras, of an infinite number. This leads to a second problem. By what *agency* have the various transformations of the primary body or bodies been produced; what is the *efficient* cause of the physical world? The early Monists ignored this problem, with the exception of the Eleatic school, who met it by asserting that change itself is a mere illusion. Parmenides, however, and the later pluralistic Physicists (Empedocles, Anaxagoras) provide some material for its solution by assigning to some elements an active, to others a passive role in the formation of things.

A further question which obviously suggests itself is the problem: What is the explanation of the presence of Order, Beauty, Goodness, and their opposites in the universe— i. e., what is the *final* cause of existence ? The first explicit recognition of such a final cause is contained in the declaration of Anaxagoras that Mind is the source of all cosmic order.

CHAPTER IV.

Still earlier implicit hints of a teleological explanation of things may be found in those writers who treat sexual Desire as a formative principle. (Hesiod, Parmenides.) Empedocles goes a step farther in recognizing Strife as well as Love as a native impulse in the universe, thus half-consciously introducing a double teleological principle, a cause of Good and a contrasted cause of Evil. But neither Anaxagoras nor Empedocles has a really consistent and well thought-out philosophy. Anaxagoras, in the actual working-out of his scheme, treats Mind as a mere mechanical agent, and only falls back upon it when he cannot find a specific physical mechanical cause of a given state of things. In Empedocles Strife is, in fact, just as much a cause of organic combinations as Love, and Love as much a source of dissolution as Strife, and though he professes to recognize four equally ultimate "elements," he really assigns a special active function to Fire and treats the other three, in contrast with Fire, as a single passive principle.

The Atomists, again, Leucippus and Democritus, consider only the problem of the *material* cause, which they solve by recognizing a pair of contrasted factors — Body, which consists of an infinity of solid atoms, and Void, or Empty Space, as the ingredients of which things are made.

CHAPTER V.

Meanwhile, the Pythagorean mathematicians were led, by fanciful analogies between the properties of numbers and those of visible things, to the view that physical things are made of numbers and that the constituent elements of number (which are the Even and Odd, or Unlimited and Limit) are the ultimate elements of the universe. In order to carry out this correspondence between numbers and things, they allowed themselves a wide license in the invention of imaginary objects. Some of them, following hints unsystematically thrown out by Alcmæon of Crotona, constructed a list of ten contrasted pairs of "opposite" principles. Their doctrine is obscure and confused, but it is clear that they meant to say that the elements of number are the *material* causes or constituent factors of things.

The Eleatics, who regarded the Universe as a simple Unity, were in consistency debarred from any inquiry into causation, since on their view all change and all processes of origination must be subjective illusions. Parmenides, however, affords some reconciliation of the Monistic doctrine with actual experience, since he seems to hold that though Being is one from the point of view of rational thought, it is many from that of sensation. Hence, in the cosmological part of his poem he treats not-Being as a causative principle opposed to and co-ordinate with Being, and thus reverts to a kind of Dualism. The cruder views of Melissus and Xenophanes call for no consideration.

Thus we see that all these philosophers recognize the existence of a *material* cause or causes, though they disagree about their number. They also recognize the existence of *efficient* causality, though some of them postulate a single initial motive impulse, others a pair of contrasted impulses. The Pythagoreans, also, adopted a dualist explanation of things, but they differed from other thinkers in holding that number and its elements are not predicates of some sensible reality, but the actual substance or stuff of which things are made. They further tentatively began to give *definitions* of some things and thus to recognize the principle of the *formal* cause, though in a crude and superficial way.

CHAPTER VI.

The system of Plato, though in general analogous to that of the Pythagoreans, has some special peculiarities. From early association with Cratylus, the Heraclitean, he derived a fixed conviction that sensible things, being essentially variable and mutable, cannot be defined. Hence, having been led by the example of Socrates to regard universal definition as the fundamental problem of science, he inferred that the objects of scientific cognition are a separate class of supra-sensible entities, which he called "Ideas," and that the corresponding classes of sensible things are connected with them by a peculiar relation which he called "participation," but the Pythagoreans "imitation." The nature of this relation was left unexplained. He further held that the objects of Mathematics form a third class of entities, intermediate between "Ideas" and sensible things. Like the "Ideas," they are immutable; like sensible things, there are many of each kind.

The "Ideas" being the causes of everything else, their constituent elements are ultimately the constituent elements of everything. These elements are two, a *material* principle, the "Great and Small," and a formal principle, the One. From the union of these two proceed the "Ideal Numbers." Thus he agreed with the Pythagoreans in holding (1) that *numbers* are the causes of all Being, and (2) that they are independent entities and not mere predicates of anything more ultimate. He differed from them in (1) taking as his material principle or Unlimited a *duality* of the "Great and Small" and (2) in regarding numbers as entities of a different kind both from sensible things and from mathematical objects.

Thus we see that this theory recognizes two forms of cause, the *formal* and the *material*. Incidentally, also, he follows the lead of Empedocles in regarding one of these factors, the One, as the cause of Good, the other as the cause of Evil.

CHAPTER VII.

We see, then, that every type of cause recognized in earlier philosophy is provided for in our fourfold classification. The *material* cause appears in one shape or another in the philosophies of Plato, the Pythagoreans, Empedocles, Anaxagoras, the Ionian Monists. The *efficient* cause has received recognition from Empedocles and Anaxagoras, not to mention the poets who have found a cosmic principle in sexual Desire. The nearest approximation to the conception of a *formal* cause or constitutive law is to be found in Platonism, according to which the Ideas constitute the *what* or essential nature of things, the One that of the Ideas. As for the *final* cause, it has in a way been recognized by Empedocles, Anaxagoras and Plato, but not in its true character. Thus our historical retrospect affords some presumption that our fourfold classification of causes is complete. It remains to point out the main defects of the various systems.

CHAPTER VIII.

Monistic Materialism (the doctrine of the Milesians Heraclitus, etc.) is defective (1) because its explanations are only applicable to corporeal things, whereas there exist also things which are incorporeal; (2) because it renders the fact of phenomenal *change* inexplicable, from its inability to recognize *efficient* causality; (3) because it ignores inquiry into the *formal* causes or constitutive laws of things; (4) because the Monistic Materialists proceed on no intelligible principle in their selection of the primary body. We may suppose other bodies to be produced from this primary body either by a process of concretion or by one of disintegration; and again, we may hold that on either view, the temporal starting-point of the process is identical with its final result, or that it is opposite. Whichever of these alternatives be adopted, we can only reasonably regard either the densest form of matter (earth) or the least dense (fire) as the primary body. The early Monists overlooked this, and selected their primary body at hap-hazard. The pluralistic materialist, Empedocles, is exposed to some of the same difficulties, and there are also special objections to his doctrine. (1) He holds that the "simple bodies" are not reciprocally convertible into each other, whereas we see, in fact, that they do pass into one another. (2) His account of efficient causality is neither correct nor consistent with itself. (3) His general position involves denial of the reality of all qualitative change. As for Anaxagoras, his doctrine of the original intermixture of all things is open, as it stands, to the following objections: (1) If such a "mixture" ever existed, there must have been a previous period during which its ingredients existed unmixed; (2) it is not true in fact that everything will "mix" with everything else; (3) what is united by "mixture" is also separable; hence, if qualities belong to things by being "mixed" with them, it should be possible to separate the "mixture" and obtain pure qualities without any corresponding substances. Probably, then, his language about the "mixture" was merely an inadequate attempt to formulate the conception of a common material substrate in physical things devoid of all determinate sensible quality. If so, his doctrine amounts to a dualism of Mind and an indeterminate Matter which closely anticipates the Platonic dualism of the One and its Other, the "Great and Small."

The doctrine of the Pythagoreans, though apparently of

a more abstract character, was also really intended as a cosmology. They too, like the early physicists just discussed, held that what *is* consists entirely of perceptible physical bodies, though their principles would really have been more in place in a system of abstract Mathematics than in Physics. They cannot possibly deduce real motion from their purely mathematical principles, nor can they give any account of the *physical* properties of body. The cosmical *causality* they ascribe to number is unintelligible if there is only one kind of numbers and these are identical with physical things.

CHAPTER IX.

To the Platonist doctrine of Ideas or "Ideal Numbers" we may object: (1) That it merely duplicates the unsolved problems of the sensible world by postulating a precisely similar "ideal" world as its counterpart. (2) The supposed proofs of the existence of Ideas are all fallacious. Some of them would require the existence of Ideas of artificial objects and of negatives, others that of Ideas of the perishable. The most exact of them lead either to the admission of Ideas of relatives or to the indefinite regress. (3) The arguments for the theory of Ideas involve assumptions inconsistent with the Platonic view of the One and the "Great and Small" as the primary elements of Being.

(4) Those arguments are also inconsistent with the theory of the "participation" of things in the Ideas. According to the former, there must be Ideas corresponding to every logical category of general names, whereas it is implied by

the doctrine of participation" that there can only be Ideas of substances.

(5) The Ideas are useless as principles for the explanation of the sensible world. (a) They do not account for our *knowledge* of the things, since, by hypothesis, they are *outside* them, in a world of their own. (b) For the same reason, they do not account for the *Being* of other things. (c) Nor do they account for the *production* of other things. "Participation," "archetype," etc., are mere empty metaphors. For who is the artist who constructs things on the model of these archetypes? Further, it will follow that there can be several archetypes of the same thing, and also that some Ideas are archetypes of other Ideas.

The mere existence of a Platonic Idea is insufficient to cause the existence of a corresponding sensible thing; and, on the other side, some things come into being of which the Platonists do not recognize *Ideas*.

(6) Special difficulties arise from the view that the Ideas are a class of *Numbers*. (a) How on such a view are we to understand the assertion that they are *causes* of sensible things? (b) What relation among Ideas corresponds to the arithmetical relations between numbers which are combined by addition into a sum? (c) The theory requires us to construct a further class of numbers which are to be the objects of arithmetic. (d) It is difficult to reconcile the assertion that the Ideas are *numbers* with the other assertion that they are *substances*.

(7) It is quite impossible to bring the fundamental con-

cepts of geometry into connection with the Platonic theory of the One and the "Great and Small" as the universal constituents of Being. Plato had seen the difficulty, so far as points are concerned, and had consequently refused to recognize their existence. But the same line of argument which establishes the existence of lines is equally valid for that of points.

(8) In short, the Ideal Theory is the substitution of mere Mathematics for Philosophy, and merely duplicates the problems of the sensible world. It throws light neither on *efficient* nor on *final* causation. Even the conception of *matter* in this philosophy is mathematical rather than physical, and, as to motion, its very existence is inconsistent with he principles of the theory. Not to mention the impossibility of finding any place whatever in the Platonic scheme for certain important geometrical entities.

(9) In general, we may say that Plato has fallen into the error of supposing that all objects of cognition are composed of the same universal elementary constituents, and that these are discoverable by analysis. But the truth is (a) that analysis into constituent elements is impossible except in the case of substances, and (b) all acquisition of knowledge presupposes previous knowledge as its basis. Hence, the Platonic conception of a single all-comprehensive science of Dialectic which analyses all objects into their elements is chimerical. Even if it were not, one could at least never be sure that the analysis had been carried to completion. Also the Platonic philosopher, who knows the elements of

everything, ought to be able to know sense-qualities without needing to have experienced the corresponding sensations.

CHAPTER X.

Thus we see that all our four significations of the term "cause" have emerged in past speculation, and no others. But the real sense and import of the principles employed has been only confusedly and dimly perceived. Even Empedocles, e. g., had a dim glimpse into the significance of *formal* causes or constitutive laws, though he was unable to give distinct expression to his thought.

CHRONOLOGICAL TABLE OF THE PRE ARISTOTELIAN PHILOSOPHERS REFERRED TO IN METAPHYSICS *A*.

B. C.

Thales   *floruit* c. 585 (he foretold the solar eclipse of this year)

Anaximander *born* c. 610

Anaximenes *floruit* c. 546

Xenophanes   "   c. 536

[Pythagoras   "   c. 532 (is said to have left Samos from disapproval of the tyranny of Polycrates)

Heraclitus   "   c. 500

Parmenides   "   c. 470 (accepting the statements of Plato in his *Parmenides*)

Empedocles   "   c. 455

Anaxagoras   *born* c. 500 d. c. 428

Melissus defeated an Athenian navy 441

Diogenes of Apollonia *floruit* c. 423 (he is satirized in the *Clouds* of Aristophanes produced that year)

Democritus   *born* c. 460 *floruit* c. 420

Socrates   "   c. 470 *died* 399

Plato   "   427 *died* 347

Where a *floruit* is given without any further explanation it is taken from the notices of the Alexandrian chronologists as preserved to us by such writers as Diogenes Laertius and Suidas. A man was conventionally assumed to be forty years old at the date of his "flourishing."

Of philosophers mentioned in the present book but not inserted in the foregoing list Hippo is known to have been a contemporary of Pericles; the physician Alcmaeon was, as Aristotle tells us, "contemporary with the old age of Pythagoras," i. e., approximately contemporary with Heraclitus. Of Hippasus nothing can be said but that he was a member of the Pythagorean order, and therefore junior to Pythagoras. Of Leucippus we can only say that he was a predecessor of Democritus and pretty certainly younger than Melissus.

As for the "Pythagoreans" mentioned by Aristotle, in the absence of names, we cannot date them precisely. The Pythagorean "Order" was violently destroyed at a date somewhere between 450 and 410, but the survivors continued to exist as a band of scientific students for some time longer. Among its later members were Philolaus of Thebes, a contemporary of Socrates, and Plato's friend Archytas, the engineer and statesman of Tarentum, probably about a generation later. See on the history of these proceedings Burnet, *op. cit.* p. 96 ff.

WORKS USEFUL TO THE STUDENT OF ARISTOTLE'S METAPHYSICS.

[I have omitted from the following list both complete editions of Aristotle's works and general histories of Greek Philosophy as a whole.]

Editions of the text of the *Metaphysics*. Commentaries, etc.

Aristotelis *Metaphysica*, edit. W. Christ. Leipzig, Teubner. 2nd edit. 1903.

Aristotelis *Metaphysica*, recognovit et emendavit Hermannus Bonitz. Bonn, 1848. (Pt. I., Text; Pt. II., Commentary in Latin.) The most important modern edition of the *Metaphysics*.

Aristoteles, *Metaphysik*, übersetzt von Hermann Bonitz. Berlin, 1890. (Posthumously edited from the papers of Bonitz by E. Wellmann.)

Alexandri Aphrodisiensis in Aristotelis *Metaphysica* Commentaria. Edit. Michael Hayduck, Berlin, 1891. (Vol. I. of the complete collection of *Commentaria in Aristotelem Græca*, published by the Berlin Academy.) Alexander of Aphrodisias in the Troad (floruit c. 200 A. D.) is far the most trustworthy of the ancient expositors of Aristotle, and the commentary on the *Metaphysics*, in particular, is an indispensable aid to the serious student of Aristotle. There is an earlier edition of the work by Bonitz, Berlin, 1847. The commentary on the first five books, with excerpts from the remainder, is also printed among the scholia in the 4th volume of the Berlin Aristotle.

General works on Aristotelian Philosophy (apart from the complete histories of Greek Philosophy).

H. Siebeck. *Aristoteles* (Frohmann's Klassiker der Philosophie, No. VIII). Stuttgart, 1899.

E. Wallace. *Outlines of the Philosophy of Aristotle.* Cambridge (Eng.) University Press, 3rd edition, 1887. A useful little digest of the main positions of the Aristotelian system, the most important passages being quoted in the original Greek at the end of each section. The student should, however, be on his guard against the author's unfortunate tendency to read Hegelianism into Aristotle.

Works on the History of Greek Philosophy down to Aristotle.

H. Ritter and L. Preller. *Historia Philosophiæ Græcæ.* 7th edition, Gotha, 1888. [Referred to in the notes to the present work as R. P.] An invaluable collection of the chief original texts for the study of Greek Philosophy, chronologically arranged.

H. Diels. *Fragmente der Vorsokratiker.* Berlin, 1903. Greek text with German translation. The latest complete critical text of the remains of the earliest Greek men of science.

H. Diels. *Doxographi Græci.* Berlin, 1879. A careful edition of the various ancient "doxographies," or summaries of the theories of philosophical schools, which can be shown to have been ultimately derived from the lost φυσικαὶ δόξαι of Theophrastus. Particularly valuable are the elaborate Prolegomena (in Latin), in which Diels placed the whole subject of the origin and value of the doxographical tradition as to the doctrines of the Pre-Socratics in an entirely new light.

A. Fairbanks. *The First Philosophers of Greece.* London, 1898. Greek text of the fragments of the Pre-Socratics with translation.

J. Burnet. *Early Greek Philosophy.* London and Edinburgh, 1892. The most important of recent English works on the Pre-Socratics, and quite indispensable to the student

Th. Gomperz. *Griechische Denker.* Leipzig, 1896. In course of publication. Vols. 1, 2, which bring the treatment of the subject down to the death of Plato, have already appeared. Vol. 1 has appeared also in an English translation under the title *Greek Thinkers.* London, 1901.

Learned and vivacious, but lacks the sound judgment of the work last mentioned.

P. Tannery. *Pour l'Histoire de la Science Hellène.* Paris, 1887. Studies of the Pre-Socratics.

G. Milhaud. *Les Philosophes-Géomètres de la Grèce: Platon et ses Prédécesseurs.* Paris 1900. A particularly valuable study of the Platonic doctrine of Ideas in the light of Greek Mathematics. The concluding chapter contains some acute examination of the anti-Platonic polemic of Aristotle's *Metaphysics*, Bks. *A* 9, *M-N*

E. Zeller. *Platonische Studien.* Tübingen, 1839. The last of the studies is an examination of Aristotle's account of Platonism.

C. Bäumker. *Das Problem der Materie in der Griechischen Philosophie.* Münster, 1890. A full and learned history of Greek philosophical theories of the nature of Matter.

The standard history of the whole development of Greek thought down to the final closing of the philosophical schools of Athens by Justinian in 529 A. D. continues to be

E. Zeller. *Philosophie der Griechen.* Last complete edition, the 4th. 5th edition in course of publication. Separate translations of various sections into English: *Pre-Socratic Philosophy*, London, 1881; *Plato and the Older Academy*, London, 1876; *Aristotle and the Earlier Peripatetics*, London, 1897.

ARISTOTLE ON HIS PREDECESSORS.

FIRST BOOK OF HIS METAPHYSICS.

ARISTOTLE ON HIS PREDECESSORS.

CHAPTER I.

All mankind have an instinctive desire of knowl- 980a 21. edge. This is illustrated by our enjoyment of our sense-perceptions. Even apart from their utility they are enjoyed for their own sake, and above all the others the perceptions of the eve. For we prize sight, speaking roughly, above everything else, not merely as a guide to action, but even when we are not contemplating any action. The reason of this is that of all the senses sight gives us most information and reveals many specific qualities.[1] Now, all animals, when they come into the world, are provided by nature with sensation, but in some of them memory does not result from their sensations, while in others 980b 21 it does. Hence the latter are both more intelligent and more able to learn than those which

---

[1] $\delta\iota\alpha\varphi\rho\dot\alpha\varsigma$; lit., "specific differences" of the various kinds of things.

are incapable of memory.[1] Creatures like the bee, and any other similar species which there may be, which cannot hear sounds, are intelligent without the power to learn; those which, in addition to memory, possess this sense *learn*.

Now, all the animals live by the guidance of their presentations[2] and memories, but only partake to a trifling degree of *experience*, but the human species lives also by the guidance of rules of art and reflective inferences. In man memory gives rise to *experience*, since repeated memories of the same thing acquire the character of a single experience. [Experience, in fact, seems to be very similar to science and art.] And science and art in man are a product of experience. For "experience has created art," as Polus correctly remarks, "but inexperience chance."[3] Art comes into being when many observations of experience give rise to a single universal conviction about a class of similar cases. Thus to be convinced that such and such a treatment was good for Callias when suffering

981 a.

---

[1] i. e., primary memory, retentiveness; *not* recall. Cf. *De Memoria*, 451a 15: "Memory is retentiveness of a presentation as an image of a presented object."

[2] φαντασίαις

[3] Reference is to Plato, *Gorgias* 448c, where Polus says: "Experience makes our life to advance by art; want of experience, by haphazard."

from such and such an ailment, and again for
Socrates, and similarly in each of many individual cases, is a result of *experience*, but the
conviction that it was found beneficial to *all*
persons of a specific constitution, whom we have
placed together as a definite class, when suffering from a specific ailment — e. g., sufferers from
catarrh, or bile, or fever — is an affair of *art*.
Now, for purposes of practice experience is recognized to be not inferior to art; indeed, we
observe that persons of experience are actually
more successful than those who possess theory
without experience. The reason of this is that
experience is acquaintance with individual facts,
but art with general rules, and all action and
production is concerned with the individual.
Thus the physician does not cure *man*, except
in an accidental sense, but Callias or Socrates or
some other individual person of whom it is an
accident to be a man. Hence, if one possesses
the theory without the experience, and is acquainted with the universal concept, but not
with the individual fact contained under it, he
will often go wrong in his treatment; for what
has to be treated is the individual.

In spite of this, however, we ascribe *knowledge*
and *understanding* to art rather than to *experience*, and regard artists as *wiser* than persons

of mere experience, thus implying that *wisdom* is rather to be ascribed to men in all cases in proportion to their *knowledge*. This is because the former class know the *reason*[1] for the thing; the latter not. Persons of mere experience know the *that,* but not the *why;* the others recognize the *why* and the reason. Hence, too, in every department master workmen are held in higher esteem and thought to know more and to be

981 b. wiser than manual workers, because they know the reasons for what is done,[2] while manual workers, it is held, are like some inanimate things which produce a result (e. g., fire *burns*), but produce it without any knowledge of it. Thus we estimate superiority in wisdom not by skill in practice, but by the possession of theory and the comprehension of reasons. In general, too, it is an indication of wisdom to be able to teach others, and on this ground, also, we regard art as more truly knowledge than experience; the artist can teach, the man of mere experience cannot. Again, we hold that none of our sense-perceptions is wisdom, though it is they which give us the most assured knowledge of individual

---

[1] or *cause* (αἰτία).

[2] The remainder of the sentence, which is not commented upon by Alexander, and interrupts the logical sequence, is not improbably a gloss.

facts. Still, they do not tell us the *reason why* about anything; e. g., they do not tell us *why* fire is hot, but merely the fact *that* it is hot. Hence it was natural that in the earliest times the inventor of any art which goes beyond the common sense-perceptions of mankind should be universally admired, not merely for any utility to be found in his inventions, but for the wisdom by which he was distinguished from other men. But when a variety of arts had been invented, some of them being concerned with the necessities and others with the social refinements of life, the inventors of the latter were naturally always considered wiser than those of the former because their knowledge was not directed to immediate utility. Hence when everything of these kinds had been already provided, those sciences were discovered which deal neither with the necessities nor with the enjoyments of life, and this took place earliest in regions where men had leisure. This is why the mathematical arts[1] were first put together in Egypt, for in that country the priestly caste were indulged with leisure.[2] (The difference between art and science

---

[1] The word "arts" ($\tau\acute{\epsilon}\chi\nu\alpha\iota$) is here used, as Bonitz notes, like the Latin *ars*, to embrace both science and art in the narrower sense.

[2] Contrast the more historical remark of Herodotus, that Egyptian geometry arose from the necessity of resurveying the land after

and the other kindred concepts has been explained in our course on Ethics; [1] the purpose of the present observations is simply to show that it is universally agreed that the object of what is called *wisdom* is first causes and principles.) So, as we have already said, the possessor of experience is recognized as wiser than the possessor of any form of sense-perception, the artist as wiser than the mere possessor of experience, the master craftsman than the manual worker, the speculative sciences than the productive. Thus it is manifest that wisdom is a form of science which is concerned with some kind of causes and principles.

982 a.

CHAPTER II.

Since we are in quest of this science, we have to ask what kind of causes and principles are treated of by the science which is wisdom? Well, the matter will perhaps become clearer if we enumerate the convictions which we currently hold about the wise man. Well, we currently

the periodical inundations of the Nile (Hdt. II., 109); and on the nature of this geometry, see Cantor, *Geschichte der Mathematik*, I., 42-73. Burnet, *Early Greek Philosophy*, 17-20.

[1] *Ethica Nicomachea*, VI., 1139b 15-1141b 23. The sentence is probably a gloss, as Christ holds.

hold, first, that the wise man, so far as possible, knows everything, but without possessing scientific knowledge of the individual details. Secondly, that he is one who is capable of apprehending difficult things and matters which it is not easy for man to apprehend; (for sense-perception is the common possession of all, and hence easy, and is nothing wise). Again, that in every science he who is more exact and more competent to teach is the wiser man. Also that, among the various sciences, that which is pursued for its own sake and with a view to knowledge has a better claim to be considered wisdom than that which is pursued for its applications, and the more commanding[1] science a better claim than the subsidiary. For the wise man, it is held, has not to be directed by others, but to direct them; it is not for him to take instructions from another, but for those who are less wise to take them from him.

Here, then, is an enumeration of our current convictions about wisdom and the wise. Now, of these marks that of *universality* of knowledge necessarily belongs to him whose knowledge has the highest generality, for in a sense he knows all that is subsumed under it. These

[1] The distinction between "commanding" and subsidiary sciences is taken from Plato, *Politicus*, 260b.

most universal truths are also in general those which it is *hardest* for men to recognize, since they are most remote from sense-perception. And the most *exact* of the sciences are those which are most directly concerned with ultimate truths. For the sciences which depend on fewer principles are more exact[1] than those in which additional assumptions are made; e. g., Arithmetic than Geometry. And, again, that science is more competent *to teach* which is more concerned with speculation on the causes of things, for in every case he who states the causes of a thing teaches. And knowledge and science *for their own sake* are found most of all in the science of that which is in the highest sense the object of knowledge. For he who chooses science for its own sake will give the highest preference to the highest science, and this is the science of that which is in the highest sense the object of knowledge. But the highest objects of knowledge are the ultimates and causes. For it is through them and as consequences of them that other truths are apprehended, not they through what is subordinate to them. And the most commanding among the sciences, more truly commanding than the subsidiary sciences, is that

982 b.

---

[1] The distinction of more and less exact sciences is again from Plato, *Philetus*, 56c ff.

which apprehends the end for which each act must be done; this end is, in each individual case, the corresponding *good*, and universally the *highest* good in the universe. All these considerations indicate that the title in question is appropriate to one and the same science. For this science must be one which contemplates ultimate principles and causes; for the good or end is itself one type of cause. That it is not a *productive* science is clear, even from consideration of the earliest philosophies. For men were first led to study philosophy, as indeed they are to-day, by *wonder*.[1] At first they felt wonder about the more superficial problems; afterward they advanced gradually by perplexing themselves over greater difficulties; e. g., the behavior of the moon, the phenomena of the sun [and stars], and the origination of the universe. Now, he who is perplexed and wonders believes himself to be ignorant. (Hence even the lover of myths is, in a sense, a philosopher, for a myth is a tissue of wonders.) Thus if they took to philosophy to escape ignorance, it is patent that they were pursuing science for the sake of knowledge itself, and not for any utilitarian applications. This

[1] An allusion to Plato, *Theaetetus*, 155d: "This emotion of wonder is very proper to a philosopher; for there is no other starting-point for philosophy."

is confirmed by the course of the historical development itself. For nearly all the requisites both of comfort and social refinement had been secured before the quest for this form of enlightenment began. So it is clear that we do not seek it for the sake of any ulterior application. Just as we call a man *free* who exists for his own ends, and not for those of another, so it is with this, which is the only *liberal*[1] science; it alone of the sciences exists for its own sake.

Hence there would be justice in regarding the enjoyment of it as superhuman. For human nature is in many respects unfree. So, in the words of Simonides,[2] "this meed belongs to God alone; for man, 'tis meet" to seek a science conformable to his estate. Indeed, if there is anything in what the poets say, and Deity is of an envious temper, it would be most natural that it should be shown here, and that all the preeminently gifted should be unlucky. But Deity cannot by any possibility be envious;[3] rather, as the proverb has it, "Many are the lies of the bards,"

983 a.

[1] The conception of "liberal" science again comes from Plato. Cf. *Republic*, VI., 499a; VII., 536e.

[2] Another Platonic reminiscence. The lines are from the poem of Simonides on Scopas, quoted in *Protagoras*, 344c.

[3] Again an echo of Plato, *Phaedrus*, 247a: "Envy has no place in the celestial choir." *Timaeus*, 29e: "He (the Creator) was good, and envy is never felt about any thing by any being who is good."

nor is it right to prize any other knowledge more highly than this. For the divinest of sciences is to be prized most highly; and this is the only science which deserves that name, for two reasons. For that science is divine which it would be most fitting for God to possess, and also that science, if there is one, which deals with divine things. And this is the only science which has both these attributes. For it is universally admitted that God is a cause and a first principle;[1] and, again, God must be thought to possess this science, either alone or in a superlative degree. To be sure, all the sciences are more indispensable, but none is nobler.

However, the acquisition of this science must in a sense lead to a condition which is the opposite of our original state of search. For, as has been said, all begin by *wondering* whether something is so,[2] just as those who have not yet examined the explanation wonder at automatic

---

[1] Hence Aristotle's own name for what his commentators called "metaphysics" is indifferently "first Philosophy" or "Theology." His doctrine of God as the supreme efficient cause is more particularly contained in book Λ (12) of the present work.

[2] Or, adopting Bonitz's proposal to transfer the words τοῖς— τὴν αἰτίαν (983a 14) and place them after πᾶσιν (a 16), "whether something is so. So men wonder at automatic marionettes, or the solstices, or the incommensurability of the diagonal. It seems, in fact, wonderful to all who have not yet examined the reason that something," etc.

marionettes. So men wonder about the solstices or the incommensurability of the diagonal.[1] It seems, in fact, a wonderful thing to everybody that something should not be measurable by any measure, even the smallest. But this wonder must end in an opposite, and, as the proverb says, a better state, as it does in these cases when knowledge has been gained. A geometer would wonder at nothing so much as he would if the diagonal were to be found commensurable.

We have explained, then, the nature of the science of which we are in quest, and the character of the end at which this inquiry and this whole branch of knowledge should aim.

CHAPTER III.

Since we manifestly must acquire scientific knowledge of ultimate causes (for in an individual case we only claim to *know* a thing when we believe ourselves to have apprehended its pri-

---

[1] i. e., the incommensurability of the diagonal of a square with its side; or, as we should say, the irrationality of $\sqrt{2}$. This was the earliest case of irrationality known to the Greeks, and was probably discovered by the Pythagoreans. The other quadratic surds from $\sqrt{3}$ to $\sqrt{17}$ were discovered by Plato's friends, Theodorus and Theaetetus (*Theaetet.*, 147d). Aristotle, who had little mathematical capacity, regularly uses "the diagonal" as his one stock illustration of incom-

mary cause), and since the term "cause" is used in four senses, to signify (1) the *essence*[1] or *essential nature*[2] of things (for the *why* is reducible in the last instance to the *concept* of the thing, but the ultimate *why* is a cause and principle), (2) the *material* or *substrate*, (3) the *source of movement*, (4) cause in a sense opposed to this last, viz., the *purpose* or *good* (for that is the end of all processes of becoming and movement),[3] though we have already treated this subject at length in our discourses on Physics, we may seek further light from the consideration of our prede- **983 b.** cessors in the investigation of Being and the philosophical examination of Reality. For they, also, obviously speak of certain principles and causes. Hence it will be of service to our present inquiry to review these principles, as we shall thus either discover some further class of causes, or be con-

---

mensurability as a non-mathematical philosopher to-day might use π. His constant recurrence to this example is perhaps explained by the prominence given to it in Plato, *Meno*, 82-84.

[1] οὐσία.

[2] τὸ τί ἦν εἶναι; lit., "What the being of the thing was found to be," i. e., the fundamental characteristics, or connotation as expressed in the definition.

[3] The scholastic names for the four senses of cause in the order of their enumeration here are thus: (1) *causa formalis*, or *forma*; (2) *causa materialis*, or *materia*; (3) *causa efficiens*; (4) *causa finalis*, or *finis*.

firmed in our confidence in the present enumeration.

Now, most of the earliest philosophers regarded principles of a *material* kind as the only principles of all things. That of which all things consist, from which they are originally generated, and into which they are finally dissolved, its substance persisting though its attributes change, this, they affirm, is an element and first principle of Being. Hence, too, they hold that nothing is ever generated or annihilated, since this primary entity[1] always persists. Similarly, we do not say of Socrates that he comes into being, in an absolute sense, when he becomes handsome or cultivated, nor that he is annihilated when he loses these qualifications, because their *substrate*, viz., Socrates himself, persists. In the same way, they held, nothing else absolutely comes into being or perishes. For there must be one or more entities[2] which persist, and out of which all other things are generated. They do not, however, all agree as to the number and character of these principles. Thales, the founder of this type of philosophy, says it is *water*. Hence,

[1] φύσις; lit., "nature." In the mouths of the early Physicists, of whom Aristotle is here speaking, the word means the supposed primary body or bodies of which all others are special modifications or transformations. (Burnet, *Early Greek Philosophy*, pp. 10-12.)

[2] φύσις; i. e., primary form of body.

he also put forward the view that the earth floats
on the water. Perhaps he was led to this conviction by observing that the nutriment of all
things is moist, and that even heat is generated
from moisture, and lives upon it. (Now, that
from which anything is generated is in every
case a first principle of it.) He based his conviction, then, on this, and on the fact that the
germs of all things are of a moist nature, while
water is the first principle of the nature of moist
things.[1] There are also some who think that
even the men of remote antiquity who first spec-
ulated about the gods, long before our own era,
held this same view about the primary entity.
For they represented Oceanus and Tethys as
the progenitors of creation, and the oath of the
gods as being by water, or, as they [the poets]
call it, Styx. Now, the most ancient of things
is most venerable, while the most venerable thing
is taken to swear by.[2] Whether this opinion

---

[1] Aristotle does not prefer to *know* the reason of Thales for his
doctrines, and the biological character of the reasons he conjecturally
ascribes to him makes it improbable, as Burnet says (*op. cit. p.* 43),
that they are really those of Thales. Possibly, as Burnet suggests,
Aristotle has, in the absence of positive information about the arguments of Thales, credited him with arguments actually employed
by Hippo of Samos, who revived his doctrine in the fifth century.

[2] Probably a "chaffing" allusion to Plato, who makes the suggestion here referred to in two obviously playful passages: *Cratylus,*
402b; *Theaetetus,* 181b.

984 a.   about the primary entity is really so original and ancient is very possibly uncertain; in any case, Thales is said to have put forward this doctrine about the first cause. (Hippo, indeed, from the poverty of his ideas, can hardly be thought fit to be ranked with such men as these.[1]) Anaximenes and Diogenes, however, regard *air* as more primitive than water, and as most properly the first principle among the elementary bodies. Hippasus of Metapontium and Heraclitus of Ephesus think it is *fire*; Empedocles, all four elements, *earth* being added as a fourth to the previous three. For they always persist and never come into being, except in respect of multitude and paucity, according as they are combined into a unity or separated out from the unity.[2] But Anaxagoras of Clazomenæ, who, though prior to Empedocles in age, was posterior[3] to him in his achievements, maintains that the number of principles is infinite. For he

---

[1] The remark about Hippo breaks the connection, and is probably, as Christ holds, a marginal gloss.

[2] Cf. Empedocles, 36 (Stein), R. P., 131b: "There is no coming into being of any perishable thing, nor any end in baneful death, but only mingling and separation of what has been mingled."

[3] "Posterior in achievements" probably means simply "later in the date of his activity as a philosopher" (Burnet). Alternative explanations are "philosophically inferior" (Alexander); "more developed in his views" (Zeller).

alleges that pretty nearly all *homœomerous*[1]
things come into being and are destroyed in this
sense [just like water and fire], viz., only by
combination and dissolution. In an absolute[2]
sense, they neither come into being nor perish, he
thinks, but persist eternally.

According to all this, one might regard the
"material" cause, as it is called, as the only kind
of cause. But as they progressed further on these
lines, the very nature of the problem pointed out
the way and necessitated further investigation.
For, however true it may be that there is underlying the production and destruction of anything
something *out of* which it is produced (whether
this be one thing or several), why does the process
occur, and what is its cause? For the substrate,
surely, is not the agent which effects its own transformation. I mean, e. g., that wood and brass
are not the causes of their respective transforma-

---

[1] "Homœomerous" things is not an expression of Anaxagoras,
but a technical term of Aristotle's own biology, denoting the forms of
organic matter (bone, flesh, etc.) which can be divided into parts of
the same character as themselves. It is here appropriately applied
to the infinity of qualitatively different molecules which Anaxagoras
regarded as the primary form of matter. (Burnet, *op. cit.* p. 289.)
The words in brackets are probably a gloss.

[2] Reading with Zeller $\dot{\alpha}\pi\lambda\tilde{\omega}\varsigma$, "in an absolute sense," for $\ddot{\alpha}\lambda\lambda\omega\varsigma$,
"in any other sense." The reference is to Anaxagoras, Fr. 17., R. P.
119: "Nothing comes into being or perishes, but there are mixture
and separation of things that already are."

tions; the wood is not the agent that makes
the bed, nor the brass the agent that makes the
statue, but something else is the cause of the
transformation. To inquire into this cause is to
inquire into the second of our principles, in my
own terminology, the *source of motion*. Now,
those who were the very first to attach themselves
to these studies, and who maintained that the
substratum was one,[1] gave themselves no trouble
over this point. Still, some[2] at least of those who
asserted its unity were, so to say, baffled by this
problem, and maintained that the one and the
universe as a whole[3] are immutable, not merely
as regards generation and destruction (for *that*
was a primitive belief in which they all concurred),
but in every other sense of the term "change;"
984 b. and this view was peculiar to them. So none
of those who said that the universe is one single
thing had an inkling of the kind of causation we
are now considering, except possibly Parmenides,
and he only recognized its existence so far as to
assume not merely one cause, but, in a sense,
two.[4] To be sure, those who assume a plurality of

---

[1] i. e., the Ionian Monists of the sixth century.

[2] Parmenides and his successors of the Eleatic School.

[3] Or "body as a whole" ($\tau\grave{\eta}\nu$ $\varphi\acute{\nu}\sigma\iota\nu$ $\~{o}\lambda\eta\nu$).

[4] The reference is to the dualistic cosmology of the second
part of Parmenides' poem, the "Way of Opinion." It is now fairly

causes are in a better position to say something on the subject; e. g., those who assume as causes heat and cold, or fire and earth, for they treat fire as having the nature of an *agent*,[1] but such things as water and earth in the opposite fashion.

After these philosophers and such first principles, since these principles were found inadequate to account for the production of the universe, men were once more compelled, as I have said, by facts themselves to investigate the principle which naturally follows next in order. For it is, perhaps, equally improbable that the reason why there are goodness and beauty both in Being and in Becoming should be fire or earth or anything else of that kind, and that these philosophers should have had such an opinion. Nor, again, would it have been reasonable to ascribe so important a result to accident and chance. So when some one said that it is the presence of *Mind* which is the cause of all order and arrangement in the universe at large, just as it is in the animal organism, he seemed, by contrast with his predecessors, like a sober man compared

established, however, that this cosmology represents the views not of Parmenides himself, but of a rival school, probably the Pythagorean, whom Parmenides regards as entirely in error. (Burnet, *op. cit.* p. 195 ff.)

[1] The reference is apparently to the active role ascribed to fire in the system of Empedocles. (Burnet, *op. cit.* p. 244.)

with idle babblers.[1] Now, we know for certain that Anaxagoras[2] had conceived this idea, but Hermotimus of Clazomenæ is alleged to have given still earlier expression to it. Those who framed this conception, then, assumed the cause of Beauty as a principle in things and, at the same time, as being a principle of the kind by which motion is communicated to things.

CHAPTER IV.

One might even fancy that this point was first investigated by Hesiod, or any other of the poets who assumed sexual Love or Desire as a principle in things — Parmenides,[3] for instance, who says, in his description of the formation of the universe: "So Love she devised as earliest-born of all the gods." So Hesiod[4] writes, "First of all things was the Abyss (χάος), and next broad-

[1] Cf. Plato's account of the effect produced upon Socrates by the famous statement of Anaxagoras about Mind, *Phaedo*, 97b ff. Aristotle probably intends an allusion to this passage.

[2] Anaxagoras, Fr. 6; R. P., 123: "All things that were to be, and that were, all things that are not now, and that are now — Mind set them all in order."

[3] Parmenides, 133; R. P., 101a. Aristotle is probably intending an allusion to Plato, *Symposium*, 178b, where both the verse of Parmenides and part of the verses from Hesiod are quoted.

[4] Hesiod. *Theogony*, 116-118.

breasted Earth, and Love conspicuous above all the immortal ones," implying that there must be in the world some cause to set things in motion and bring them together. (How the question of priority is to be settled between these authors is a point of which we may be allowed to postpone the consideration.) But, further, since it was patent that there is also present in the universe the opposite of good, and not only Order and Beauty, but also Disorder and Ugliness, and that the evil and unseemly things are more numerous than the good and beautiful, another poet introduced the concepts of Love[1] and Strife as the respective causes of each class. For if one follows out the statements of Empedocles with attention to his meaning, and not to its lisping expression in words, it will be found that he treats Love as the cause of good things, Strife as the cause of evil. Hence, if one said that in a sense Empedocles designated, and was the first to designate, Good and Evil as principles, the remark would probably be just, since that which is the cause of all good things is the *Good* itself [and that which is the cause of all evil things is *Evil* itself].

985 a.

---

[1] φιλία, "affection," "mutual attraction." Empedocles (for whom see Burnet, *op. c.t.* pp. 245-247) uses for the principle of attraction the names of φιλίτης (= Aristotle's φιλία) and Aphrodite (= Aristotle's ἔρως, sexual attraction) indifferently.

As I have said, then, the writers just referred to manifestly had formed the conception, to the degree already indicated, of two of the senses of Cause which have been distinguished in my discourses on Physics—the Matter and the Source of Motion. Their exposition, however, was obscure and confused, and might be likened to the conduct of untrained recruits in battle. In the general mêlée such recruits often deal admirable blows, but they do not deal them with science. Similarly, these philosophers do not seem to understand the significance of their own statements, for it is patent that, speaking generally, they make little or no application of them. Anaxagoras, for instance, uses his "Mind" as a mechanical[1] device for the production of order in Nature, and when he is at a loss to say by what cause some result is necessitated, then he drags in Mind as a last resource, but in all other cases he assigns anything and everything rather than Mind as the cause of what occurs.[2] Empedocles, again, though he makes more use of his causes than

---

[1] μηχανῇ. The metaphor is from the machine used in the theatre to hoist up the god who appears to "cut the knot" of an otherwise insoluble dramatic tangle. The idiomatic English rendering would be: "He treats Mind as a sort of fairy godmother."

[2] An obvious allusion to the complaint of Socrates in Plato, Phaedo, 98b. ff: "As I went on to read further, I found that the

the other, does not make adequate use of them,
nor does he succeed in attaining consistency where
he does employ them. At least, he frequently
treats Love as a separating and Strife as a com-
bining agency.[1]   Thus, when the Universe is
resolved into its rudiments[2] by Strife, fire and each
of the other four are combined into one, but when
they coalesce again into the One, under the influence of Love, the parts of each are necessarily
separated again.   Empedocles, then, differed from
his predecessors in being the first to introduce
this cause in a *double* form; he assumes, not a
single source of motion, but a pair which are opposed to one another. He was also the first to
assert that the number of the so-called material

man made no use of his 'Mind,' and assigned no real causes for the
order in things, but alleged as causes airs, ethers, waters, and a host
of other monstrosities."

[1] For this criticism, cf. *Metaphysics, B,* 1000a 26: "It is true
that he assumes a certain principle as the cause of dissolution,
viz., Strife.   But one has to suppose that Strife just as truly *produces*
everything except the One."   For a full commentary on this, see
Burnet, *op. cit.* p. 246.

[2] στοιχείων.   The word, which primarily means a letter of the
alphabet, is taken by Aristotle from Plato, *Theaetetus,* 201e ff, where
the analysis of a complex into its simple factors is illustrated by the
spelling of a syllable.   Aristotle's definition of στοιχεῖον, which I
shall henceforth render "element," is (*Metaphysics, Δ* 3, 1014a 26) "an
ultimate factor present in a complex, not further divisible in respect of
its kind into factors which differ in kind."   The term was, of course,
unknown to Empedocles, whose name for his "elementary bodies"
is simply "roots of things."

elements is four. Yet, he does not employ them as four, but as if they were only two, treating fire on the one side by itself, and the elements

985 b. opposed to it—earth, air, and water—on the other, as if they were a single nature. One can discover this from his verses by careful reflection. Such, then, were the nature and number of the principles assumed by Empedocles.

But Leucippus and his follower, Democritus, say that the elements are the Full and the Void, calling the one Being and the other Non-being. The full and solid they call Being, the void and rare Non-being. (This, too, is why they say that Non-being is just as real as Being, for the Void is as real as Body.[1]) These are, they declare, the *material* causes of things. And just as those who regard the underlying nature of things as one derive everything else from the modifications of this substrate, assuming density and rarity as the fundamental distinction between these modifications, so Leucippus and Democritus assert that the *differences*[2] are the causes of everything else. Now, of these they say there are three—

---

[1] The Greek text has "for Body is real as Void." The context shows that we must emend the reading of the MS. into the sense given above. The simplest method of doing this is, with Zeller, to substitute ἔλαττον for μᾶλλον in 985b 8.

[2] i. e., the differences between the atoms of which according to this school Being, or Body, is composed.

shape, order, and position. For Being, they say, differs only in *contour* (ῥυσμός), *arrangement* (διαθιγή), *situation* (τροπή). Of these terms, *contour* means shape, *arrangement* means order (διαθιγή), and *situation* means position.[1] Thus, e. g., A differs from N in shape, AN from NA in order, Z from N in position. Like the rest of the philosophers, they also indolently neglected the question whence or how motion is communicated to things. This, then, is the point to which the investigation of these two kinds of cause seems to have been carried by the earlier thinkers.

CHAPTER V.

At the same time, and even earlier, the so-called Pythagoreans attached themselves to the mathematics and were the first to advance that science[2] by their education, in which they were

---

[1] Aristotle explains the unfamiliar technical expressions of the Atomists, which are all words belonging to their native Ionic dialect, by Attic equivalents. I fear my attempt to find unfamiliar synonyms for such common technical terms as shape, order, position is not altogether happy, but it is the best I can do. Z is said below to differ from N only in position because it is the same figure rotated through a right angle. The paleographical correction of this sentence by Diels does not affect the sense, and I have therefore been content to keep the traditional text.

[2] On the nature and extent of the Pythagorean mathematics, see particularly Cantor, *Geschichte der Mathematik*, I., pp. 137-160

led to suppose that the principles of mathematics are the principles of all things. So as *numbers* are logically first among these principles, and as they fancied they could perceive in numbers many analogues of what is and what comes into being, much more readily than in fire and earth and water (such and such a property of number being *justice*, such and such another *soul* or *mind*, another *opportunity*, and so on, speaking generally, with all the other individual cases), and since they further observed that the properties and determining ratios of *harmonies* depend on numbers—since, in fact, everything else manifestly appeared to be modelled in its entire character on numbers, and numbers to be the ulti-

986 a. mate[1] things in the whole Universe, they became convinced that the elements of numbers are the elements of everything, and that the whole "Heaven"[2] is harmony and number. So, all the

Milhaud, *Les Philosophes-Géomètres de la Grèce*, bk. 1, ch. 2.   Note that Aristotle never professes to know anything of the philosophical or scientific views of Pythagoras himself. On the sources of his knowledge of the "so-called Pythagoreans," consult Burnet, *op. cit.* p. 321.

[1] πρῶτοι; literally, "first," as above.

[2] οὐρανός; literally, "heaven" meant to the early Greek physicists the whole collection of bodies comprised within the apparent vault of the sky. We must not translate by "universe," since it was commonly held that much which exists is outside the οὐρανός. An equivalent term of later date, probably of Pythagorean origin, is κόσμος.

admitted analogies they could show between numbers and harmonies and the properties or parts of the "Heaven" and the whole order of the universe, they collected and accommodated to the facts; if any gaps were left in the analogy, they eagerly caught at some additional notion, so as to introduce connection into their system as a whole. I mean, e. g., that since the number 10 is thought to be perfect, and to embrace the whole essential nature of the numerical system, they declare also that the number of revolving heavenly bodies is ten, and as there are only nine[1] visible, they invent the Antichthon as a tenth. But I have discussed this subject more in detail elsewhere.[2] I only enter on it here for the purpose of discovering from these philosophers as well as from the others what principles they assume, and how those principles fit into our previous classification of causes. Well, they, too, manifestly regard number as a principle, both in the sense that it is the *material* of things, and in the sense that it constitutes their *properties* and *states*. The elements of number are, they think, the Even and the Odd, the former being unlimited, the latter limited. Unity is

[1] viz., Earth, Moon, Sun, Mercury, Venus, Mars, Jupiter, Saturn, circle of Fixed Stars.

[2] In a now lost work, "*On the Pythagoreans.*"

composed of both factors, for, they say, it is both even and odd. Number is derived from unity, and numbers, as I have said, constitute the whole "Heaven."

Other members of the same school say that the principles are ten, which they arrange in a series of corresponding pairs:[1]

Limit — the Unlimited.
Odd — Even.
Unity — Multitude.
Right — Left.
Male — Female.
Rest — Motion.
Straight — Curved.
Light — Darkness.
Good — Evil.
Square — Oblong.

Alcmæon of Crotona appears to have followed the same line of thought, and must either have borrowed the doctrine from them or they from

[1] On the meaning of this numerical cosmology of the Pythagoreans the student will find most enlightenment in the works of Burnet and Milhaud, previously referred to, and the section on Pythagoreanism in Bäumker, *Das Problem der Materie in der Griechischen Philosophie.* He should note, also, the fundamental initial error which vitiated all ancient arithmetical theory, viz., the view that 1, and not 0, is the first of the series of integers. This view is connected partly with the defects of Greek arithmetical notation, partly with an erroneous assumption, tacitly made by all Greek logicians, as to the "existential import" of predication.

him, since Alcmæon was contemporary with the
old age of Pythagoras. His views were very
similar to theirs. He says, in fact, that most
things human form pairs, meaning pairs of opposites. He does not, however, like the Pythagoreans, give a precise list of these, but mentions
at random any that occur to him, e. g., White-
Black, Sweet-Bitter, Good-Bad, Great-Small.
Thus in other cases he merely threw out indefinite
suggestions, but the Pythagoreans further under- **986 b**
took to explain how many and what the oppo-
sites are. From both, then, we can learn this much:
that the opposites are the principles of things,
but only from the latter how many, and what
these are. They have not clearly explained in
detail how these opposites are to be reduced to
our previous classification of causes, but they
appear to treat their elements as the *material* of
things; for they say that Being[1] is composed and
fashioned out of them as inherent constituent
factors. The meaning, then, of those ancients
who asserted that the elements of the universe
are a plurality can be sufficiently perceived from
the foregoing exposition. But there are some[2]
who expressed the view that the all is one single
entity, though they differed among themselves

[1] $\tau\grave{\eta}\nu$ $o\vartheta\sigma\acute{\iota}a\nu$.
[2] viz , the Eleatics.

both in respect of the merits of their doctrine, and in respect of its logical character. Now, a discussion of their views is not strictly relevant to our present inquiry into causation, for, unlike some of the physicists[1] who postulate the unity of Being, and yet treat of its derivation from the one substance as its material cause, they maintain the doctrine in a different sense. Those physicists assume, also of course, the existence of *motion*, since they treat of the *derivation* of the All, but this school declares that the All is motionless. Still, one observation at least is relevant to our present inquiry. Parmenides appears to conceive of the One in a formal sense, Melissus in a material. Hence the former calls it limited, the latter unlimited. Xenophanes, who was the first of them to teach the doctrine of unity (for they say that Parmenides had been his disciple), did not make any definite pronouncement, and seems to have formed the notion of neither of these entities, but gazing up at the whole Heaven[2], declared that the One is God. As I said, then, for the purposes of the present investigation this school may be disregarded. Two of them we may disregard altogether as a little too naïve,[3]

---

[1] i. e., the Ionian Monists, from Thales to Heraclitus.

[2] Or, perhaps, "contemplating the Universe as a whole."

[3] "Naïveté" (ἀγροικία) is a technical term with Aristotle,

viz., Xenophanes and Melissus, but Parmenides appears, perhaps, to speak with greater insight. For, since he claims that Non-being, as contrasted with Being, is nothing, he is forced to hold that Being is one, and that nothing else exists—a doc-- trine on which we have spoken more fully and clearly in our course on Physics.[1] But, as he is obliged to adapt his views to sensible appear- ances, he assumes that things are one from the point of view of reason, but many from that of sensation, and thus reintroduces a duality of principles and causes, the Hot and Cold, by which he means, e. g., fire and earth. Of these he co-ordinates the Hot with Being, its counter-- **987 a.** part with Non-being.

Now, from the account we have just given, and by a comparison of the thinkers who have previously concerned themselves with the sub- ject, we have arrived at the following result. From the earliest philosophers we have learned of a bodily principle (for water, fire, and the

for want of acquaintance with formal logic. On the particular logical fallacy to which he objected in Melissus, see Burnet, *op. cit.* p. 341, and on his misapprehension of the second part of the poem of Parmenides, p. 195 of the same work. Plato, it should be said, held the same view as to the relative merits of these two philosophers. See *Theaetetus,* 183e.

[1] *Physics*, I., 3, 186a 3, ff.

like, are bodies), which some of them[1] regard
as a single principle, others[2] as a plurality, though
both schools treat these principles as bodily.
From others we have learned, in addition to this
principle, of a source of motion, and this also
is regarded by some[3] of them as one, but by
others[4] as twofold. They all, down to the Italian[5]
school and exclusive of them, treated the subject in a rather ordinary[6] way. As I have said,
they only employed two kinds of cause, and the
second of these, the source of motion, some of
them regarded as one, others as two. The Pythagoreans likewise maintained a duality of principles, but they added, and this is peculiar to them,
the notion that the limited, the unlimited, the
one are not predicates of some other entity, such
as fire, or earth, or something else of that kind,
but that the Unlimited and the One themselves are
the *substance* of the things of which they are predi-

---

[1] The Milesians, Heraclitus, Diogenes.

[2] Empedocles, Anaxagoras, the Atomists.

[3] i. e., Anaxagoras.

[4] i. e., Empedocles.

[5] i. e., the Pythagoreans of Magna Græcia

[6] $\mu\epsilon\tau\rho\iota\dot{\omega}\tau\epsilon\rho\sigma\nu$.   If the text is correct, this must mean "un-
satisfactorily," though the word will hardly bear that sense.   There
is a rival MS. reading $\mu\alpha\lambda\alpha\chi\dot{\omega}\tau\epsilon\rho\sigma\nu$, "rather feebly," and Alexander of
Aphrodisias appears to be explaining a reading $\mu\sigma\nu\alpha\chi\dot{\omega}\tau\epsilon\rho\sigma\nu$, "rather
one-sidedly."

cated. This is why, according to them, number is the *substance* of everything.

This was the doctrine they proclaimed on
these points. They also began to discuss the
what of things, and to give definitions of it, but
their method of procedure was extraordinarily
crude. Their definitions were superficial, and
they regarded anything to which a term under
examination first applied as the essential nature
of the object in question, as if one were to think
that "double of" and "the number 2" are the
same thing, on the ground that 2 is the first
number which is double of another. But, methinks,
it is not the same thing to be double of something
as it is to be the number 2. If it were, then one
thing would be many[1], a consequence which
actually followed in their system.[2] So much,
then, is what may be learned from the earlier
thinkers and their successors.

[1] For, if every number which is double of another *is* the number 2
the single number 2 must be identical with an infinity of other even
numbers, 4, 6, 8. . . .

[2] The, way in which this occurred was that the same number was
identified, on the strength of different fanciful analogies, with a variety
of different objects. Thus 1 was "the point," but it was also "the
soul."

CHAPTER VI.

The said philosophies were succeeded by the system of Plato, which was for the most part in harmony with them, but had also some distinctive peculiarities by which it was discriminated from the philosophy of the Italians[1]. In his youth Plato had been familiar with Cratylus and with the Heraclitean doctrines, according to which all things perceived by the senses are in incessant flux, and there is no such thing as scientific knowledge of them, and to this part of the doctrine he remained true through life.

987 b. Socrates, however, though confining his examination to questions of moral conduct, and giving no study to the nature of the universe as a whole, sought within the moral sphere for the universal, and was the first to concentrate his attention on definitions. Hence Plato, who succeeded him, conceived for the reason immediately to be mentioned that the objects thus defined cannot be any sensible things, but are of some different kind, since it is impossible that there should be a general definition of a sensible thing, as such things are incessantly changing. Hence he called this kind of things "Ideas," and held that all sensible

[1]. e., the Pythagoreans.

things exist by the side of them and are named after them; for the multiplicity of things called by the same names as the Ideas exist, he holds, in consequence of their "participation" in them.[1]

In this theory of participation the only innovation lay in the name, for the Pythagoreans say that things exist by "imitation" of the numbers, and Plato by "participation" [a mere change of a word]. But what this "participation in" or "imitation of" the Ideas may be, they left for their successors to inquire.

Further, he teaches that the objects of mathe-

[1] Cf. the fuller parallel passage, *Metaphysics*, *M*, 1078a 9 ff: "The theory of Ideas arose in the minds of its originators from their persuasion of the truth of the Heraclitean doctrine, that all sensible things are always in flux. Hence, they inferred, if there is to be scientific knowledge and rational comprehension of anything, there must be other entities distinct from those of sense, and they must be permanent. Now, Socrates confined his studies to the moral virtues, and was the first to attempt universal definition in connection with them. Among the physicists, Democritus had indeed just touched the fringe of the problem, and had given a sort of definition of heat and cold, and the Pythagoreans even earlier had discussed the definition of a few concepts, connecting them with their theory of numbers. They asked, e. g., what is opportunity, or justice, or marriage? But Socrates had a good reason for inquiring into the *what* of things. He was attempting to construct syllogisms, and the 'what is it' is the starting-point of the syllogism. . . . There are, in fact, two things which must in justice be assigned to Socrates, inductive arguments and universal definition. For both of these have to do with the foundation of science. Socrates, however, did not regard his universals, or definitions, as separable from things; his successors made the separation, and called this class of objects 'Ideas.'"

matics exist as an intermediate class beside the
Ideas and sensible things. They differ from
sensible things in being eternal and immutable,
and from the Ideas in this, that there is a multiplicity of similar mathematical objects, but each
Idea is a single, self-subsisting entity.[1]

And since the Ideas are the causes of everything else, he thought that their constituent elements are the elements of everything. Their
material principle, then, is the "Great and
Small," but their formal principle the One.
For the numbers [which are the Ideas][2] are
derived from the former principle by participation in the One. In regarding the One as a
substance, and not as a predicate of some other
entity, his doctrine resembles Pythagoreanism,
and also in holding that the numbers are the
causes of Being in everything else. But it is

[1] From the polemic against Plato, which occupies books M and
N of the *Metaphysics*, particularly from M 2, 1076b, it appears that
Aristotle understood Plato to distinguish between three kinds of
entity, each of which is in its ultimate constitution a number, or ratio
of numbers: (1) The *sensible* object, e. g., a visible round disc; (2) the
"mathematical object," e. g., our visual imagination of a perfectly
circular disc; (3) the *Idea*, e. g., *the* circle in the sense in which it is
studied by the analytical geometer, and defined by its equation. (2)
differs from (3) as "circles" from "*the* circle."

[2] The text is τὰ εἴδη τοὺς ἀριθμούς, where either τὰ εἴδη or
τοὺς ἀριθμούς is pretty clearly a gloss. I follow Zeller's reading.
Christ has τὰ εἴδη [τοὺς ἀριθμούς], "the Ideas [which are the
numbers]."

peculiar to him to set up a duality instead of the single Unlimited, and to make the Unlimited consist of the Great and Small.[1] It is a peculiarity, also, that he regards the Numbers as distinct from sensible things, whereas the Pythagoreans say that things themselves *are* number, and do not assert the existence of an intermediate class of mathematical objects. This treatment of the One and the Numbers as distinct from things, in which he differed from the Pythagoreans, and also the introduction of the "Ideas," were due to his logical[2] studies (for his predecessors knew nothing of Dialectic); his conception of the second principle as a Duality, to the ease with which numbers other than primes can be generated from such a Duality as a matrix.[3] **988 a.**

[1] This "Great and Small," or principle of indefinite, variability, is regularly spoken of by Aristotle in the sequel as "the indeterminate Dyad" or "Duality." It corresponds exactly to the notion of "the variable" in modern Logic and Mathematics. The nearest equivalent phrase in the writings of Plato himself occurs at *Philebus*, 24e, where the ἄπειρον or indeterminate is characterized as "all things which appear to us to exist in a greater and a less degree, and admit the qualifications 'intensely,' 'gently,' 'excessively' and the like." According to the ancient commentators, the foregoing account of the composition of the Ideas, which is not to be found explicitly in any of the Platonic writings, was given orally by Plato in lectures which were posthumously edited by Aristotle and others of his disciples.

[2] τὴν ἐν τοῖς λόγοις σκέψιν, "his inquiries in the domain of concepts," i. e., his study of the nature of logical definition and division.

[3] A matrix, ἐκμαγεῖον; properly, a mass of material pre-

Yet, the actual process is the reverse of this, and his suggested derivation has no logical foundation. According to his followers, the existence of a multiplicity of things is a consequence of matter, whereas each Form is only productive once for all. Yet, it is notorious that only one table[1] can be fashioned from one and the same piece of timber, whereas he who impresses the form on it, though but a single workman, can make many tables. So with the relation of the

pared to receive a mould or stamp, a Platonic term borrowed by Aristotle from *Theaetetus*, 191c; *Timaeus*, 50c. The clause "other than primes" is difficult to interpret, and has been treated as a mistaken gloss. I think, however, that it alludes to *Parmenides*, 143–4, where Plato deduces from the existence of 1, that of 2, and from these two that of the whole series of all the other integers which can be resolved into factors, whether odd or even; i. e., all *except* the primes. If this explanation is correct, and it appears to have been held by Bonitz (see his edition of the *Metaphysics*, Commentary, p. 94-5), this is one of several passages which refute the current assertion that the dialogue *Parmenides* is never cited by Aristotle. Another is *N*, 1091a 11, which unmistakably refers to the same passage of the *Parmenides*. It should, however, be observed that the two factors from which numbers are derived in that dialogue are not the number 1 and the Variable or "*Indeterminate* Duality," but the number 1, and *the number* 2, "the *Ideal* Duality." This conscious or unconscious perversion of Plato's theory of numbers recurs throughout the whole of the sustained polemic of Books *M, N*.

[1] The illustration of the table is an echo of *Republic*, X., 596a. Aristotle is punning on the literal meaning of the word ὕλη, *timber*, which he employs as a technical term for the "material" from which a thing is produced.

male to the female; the latter is impregnated by a single coition, but one male can impregnate many females. And yet these relations are "copies" of those principles!

This, then, is the account which Plato gave of the questions we are now investigating. From our statement it is clear that he only employed two kinds of cause, the principle of the *what* and the material cause. (The Ideas, in fact, are the cause of the *what* in everything else, and the One in the Ideas themselves.) He also tells us what is the material substratum of which the Ideas are predicated in the case of sensible things, the One in the case of the Ideas, viz., that it is the duality of the "Great and Small." He further identified these two elements with the causes of good and evil, respectively, a line of research which, as we have said, had already been followed by some of his philosophical predecessors, e. g., Empedocles and Anaxagoras.

CHAPTER VII.

We have now summarily and in outline answered the questions, what thinkers have treated of principles and of reality, and what doctrines they have taught. This much, however, can be gathered from our sketch of them, viz., that of all who have discussed principles and causes none has spoken of any kind except those which have been distinguished in our discourses on Physics. They are all unmistakably, though obscurely, trying to formulate these. Some of them understand their principle in the sense of a *material* cause, whether this be regarded as one or as several, as a body or as something incorporeal. E. g., Plato, with his Great and Small; the Italians, with their Unlimited; Empedocles, with his fire, earth, water, and air; Anaxagoras, with the infinity of his homœomerous bodies. All these, then, have formed the concept of cause in this sense, as likewise all those who make a first principle of air,[1] or fire,[2] or water,[3] or a body denser than fire but finer than air;[4] for, in fact, some have identified the prime element with such a body. These thinkers, then, apprehended only this form of cause; others had apprehended cause, also, in the sense of the source of motion, e. g., those who make a principle of Love and Strife,

[1] Anaximenes, Diogenes.

[2] Heraclitus.

[3] Thales (Hippo).

[4] On the identification of the philosopher thus designated, see Burnet, *op. cit.* 56-58, and references given there. I hold with Burnet that the criticism of the doctrine in *De Coelo*, 303b 12, proves that the allusion is to Anaximander.

or Mind, or sexual Love. The *what* [1] or essential nature[2] has not been explicitly assigned by any of them, but the authors of the theory of Ideas have come nearest to recognizing it. For they neither conceive the Ideas as the *material* of sensible things and the One as that of the Ideas, nor do they regard them as providing the source of motion (indeed, they say that they are rather causes of motionlessness and rest), but the *what* [1] is supplied to everything else by the Ideas, and to the Ideas by the One. The end *for the sake of which* actions, changes, and movements take place they do, in a sense, introduce as a cause, but not in this form, nor in one corresponding to its real character. For those who speak of Mind or Love assume these causes, indeed, as something good, but not in the sense that anything is or comes to be *for the sake of them*, but only in the sense that motions are initiated by them. Similarly, those[3] who assert that Being, or the One, are entities of this kind[4] assert, indeed, that they are a cause of existence, but not that anything is or comes to be *for the sake of them*. Consequently they, in a sense, both assert and deny that the Good is a

[1] τὸ τί ἦν εἶναι.

[2] τὴν οὐσίαν.

[3] i. e., Plato and his followers.

[4] i. e., Sources of motion.

cause, for they treat it as such, not absolutely but *per accidens*.[1] They all thus appear to supply evidence that our own determination of the number and kind of the senses of cause is correct, since they have all failed to conceive of any further sense of cause. Further, it is clear that we must investigate these principles either as they stand in their entirety or a selection of them. We will next, however, examine possible difficulties in the doctrines of the individual thinkers, and their views about principles.

CHAPTER VIII.

It is clear, then, that all who regard the universe as one and assume a single entity as its material, and that a bodily and extended[2] entity, have fallen into error in several respects. They only assume constituent elements for bodies, but not for incorporeal entities, though incorporeal entities also really exist, and though they attempt to provide

---

[1] i. e., they treat "the Good" as being a cause only in a relative and derivative sense, because it happens also to be something which *mechanically* initiates movement.

[2] $\mu \acute{\epsilon} \gamma \epsilon \theta o \varsigma$ $\H{\epsilon} \chi o \upsilon \sigma a \nu$; lit., "having magnitude." $\mu \acute{\epsilon} \gamma \epsilon \theta o \varsigma$ (see Bonitz's *Index Aristotelicus sub. voc.*) means to Aristotle *res extensa, spatial* magnitude, whether purely geometrical or physical.

causes for generation and dissolution, and to discuss the nature of all things, they do away with the cause of motion. A further fault is that they do not assume the essential nature,[1] or *what*, as a cause of anything. Another is the levity with which they call any one of the simple bodies except earth a principle, without reflection on the process of their reciprocal generation from each other. [I am speaking of fire, water, earth, and air.] Some of them are generated from one another by composition, others by separation, and this difference is of the highest importance in deciding the question of priority and posteriority. From one point of view, one might hold that the most elementary of things is that out of which they are all ultimately generated by composition, and such would be the body which is finest in texture and has the minutest parts. Hence those who **989 a.** assume fire as their principle would be most fully in accord with this line of thought, and even each of the others admits that the *element* of bodies must be of this kind; at least, none of the later thinkers who asserted a single principle has ventured to say that this element is earth — the reason clearly being the great size of its parts — though each of the three other elements has found an advocate. For some identify the primary element

[1] τὴν οὐσίαν.

with fire, others with water, others with air. And yet why do they not say the same thing about earth, too, just as the mass of mankind do? And Hesiod,[1] too, says that earth was the first of bodies, so primitive and popular is this belief found to be.

According to this line of thought, then, whether a man says that the primary body is any one of these other than fire or assumes that it is denser than air but finer than water, he cannot be right in either case. But if what is sequent in the order of production is logically anterior,[2] then, since the compacted and composite comes later in the order of production, we should have an opposite conclusion to the above: water would be prior to air; earth, to water.

So much, then, may be said about those who postulate a single cause of this kind. The same criticisms are pertinent, even if one assumes a plurality of them, like Empedocles, who says that the material of things is four bodies. The same consequences must follow in his system, as well

---

[1] In the passage previously referred to, *Theogony*, 116 ff.

[2] τῇ φύσει πρότερον, "prior in the order of *nature*," it being a doctrine of Aristotle, ultimately based upon his biological studies, that the completed result of a process of development is presupposed by, and therefore logically, and in the end temporally also, prior to its incomplete stages. For the different senses of priority and posteriority, see *Metaphysics*, Δ 11.

as others peculiar to it. For we see these bodies
produced from one another, and this implies that
fire and earth do not always remain the same body,
a point which has been discussed in our discourses
on Physics[1]. And, further, he cannot be thought
to have spoken with entire correctness or consistency on the question whether the cause of motion
is to be assumed to be single or double. And universally those who teach this doctrine are forced
to deny the reality of qualitative alteration.
Nothing will become cold after being hot, or hot
after being cold. For there would need to be
something to be the subject of these contrasted
states. And thus there would be a numerically
single entity which becomes successively fire and
water; but this *he* denies.

As for Anaxagoras, he would be most rationally
interpreted if we understood him to recognize two
elements. He did not, indeed, develop this notion
himself, but would necessarily have followed another's guidance in this direction. That all things
were at first a mixture[2] is indeed a paradoxical

---

[1] Reference is to *De Cælo*, III., 7; *De Generatione*, II., 6.

[2] The reference is to Anaxagoras. Fr. (1) "All things were together, infinite both in number and smallness," etc.; Fr. (4) "Before
the separating off, when all things were together, there was not even
any colour perceptible, for the commingling of all things forbade it,"
etc.; R. P., 120: "But *Mind* is . . . not mingled with anything;" Fr.
(6), R. P., 123.

989 b.

view on various grounds, particularly because it follows that they would first have to exist in an unmixed state, and also because it is not the nature of anything and everything to admit of mixture with everything else. Besides, the attributes and accidents of things would be separable from their substances (since things which can mix can also be separated). Still, if one followed up his doctrine and developed his meaning, he would perhaps be found to be asserting a view more akin to that of later thinkers. For when nothing had been separated off, clearly nothing could be truly predicated of the supposed substance. I mean, e. g., that it could not be truly called white, black, buff [nor of any other color], but must necessarily have been colorless, since otherwise it would have had one or the other of these tints. Similarly, for the same reason it could have no taste, nor any other such quality. It could neither have been a quality, nor a quantity, nor a thing. If it had been, it would have had the form of some definite particular thing. But this is impossible, on the assumption that all things were mixed together, for it would be equivalent to being already separated out. But he says that all things were mixed together except Mind, which alone was unmixed and pure. It follows, then, from all this that his theory amounts to assigning as his principles the One (for that is simple and unmixed), and the Other, as we[1] call the Indeterminate before it has been rendered determinate and received a form. Thus what he says is neither correct nor clear; still, what he means is something similar to later theories and more conformable to apparent facts.

These thinkers, however, confine themselves exclusively to the study of generation, dissolution, and motion, for in general they inquire exclusively about the causes and principles of that kind of Being. As for those who study all forms of Being, and distinguish between sensible and non-sensible objects, they clearly devote their attention to both classes. Hence, in their case, we may dwell at rather greater length on the question what satisfactory or unsatisfactory contributions they have made to the solution of the problems at present before us.

The so-called Pythagoreans, then, employ less obvious principles and elements than the physicists (the reason being that they did not derive them from *sensible* things; for mathematical objects, with the exception of those with which astronomy is concerned, are devoid of motion).

---

[1] "We"—i. e., the school of Plato. Throughout the present discussion Aristotle affects to speak as a critic of Plato from within the Platonic circle, a point of which we shall see further illustration in ch. IX.

990 a.

Still, all their discussions and investigations are concerned with physical Nature. For they describe the formation of the "Heaven," and observe what befalls its parts [attributes and activities], and use up their causes and principles upon this task, which implies that they agree with the other physicists, that *what is* is just so much as is perceptible by our senses and comprised by the so-called "Heaven." Yet, as I have said, the causes and principles they assign are adequate for the ascent to the higher classes of entities,[1] and, indeed, more appropriate to these than to the science of Physics. But they fail to explain how there can be motion if all that we presuppose in our premises is merely Limit, the Unlimited, the Odd and the Even, or how without Motion and Change there can be Generation, and Dissolution, or the actions of the bodies that traverse the "Heaven."[2]

Again, even if it were granted them or proved that *magnitude*[2] is composed of these factors, how does this account for the existence of *bodies*, light

---

[1] "higher"—i. e., requiring a greater degree of generalising abstraction for their comprehension; in Aristotle's favorite phrase, "farther removed from sense."

[2] i. e., *Res extensa*, Body, conceived in a purely geometrical fashion and denuded of all *physical* properties. Aristotle's point is, that just because the Pythagoreans (like Descartes after them) conceived of Body in purely geometrical terms they could give no explanation of its sensible physical properties.

and heavy? For they reason from the principles they assume just as much about sensible as about mathematical bodies. Hence they have not taught us anything about fire or earth or other such bodies, and naturally not, as they had no special doctrine about sensible objects as such. Again, how can we understand the view that Number and its properties are the causes of all that is and that comes to be in the "Heaven," both at the beginning and now, and yet that there is no other kind of number than this Number of which the universe is composed? For when, according to them, there is in this region of the universe Opinion and Opportunity, and a little higher or lower Injustice and Separation or Mixture, and when they say as a proof of this that each of these is a number, and when it also comes about that there is already in this region a collection of composite[1] magnitudes, because these properties are attached each to a particular region — is it the same number as that in the "Heaven," which we are to suppose to be each of these things, or some other kind of number?[2] Plato, to be sure,

[1] i. e., extended figures or bodies (the Pythagoreans did not distinguish the two), which, according to them, are "composed" of the numerical factors, Limit, the Unlimited.

[2] In this difficult sentence I have followed the reading and interpretation of Burnet, *op. cit.* p. 316, which differs from that of Christ in the following points: 990a 25, omit μέν and, with Bonitz, read συμβαίνῃ

says it is a different kind, though he, too, thinks that both these things[1] and their causes are numbers, but believes that the causative numbers are perceived by thought, the other kind by sense.

CHAPTER IX.

For the present, then, we may dismiss the subject of the Pythagoreans; the foregoing brief mention of them will be found adequate. As for

990 b.   those who assume the Ideas as causes, in the first

for συμβαίνει; line 28, omit οὗτος, with the MS Ab), though this last change is perhaps unnecessary. The general meaning is, then, as follows: Besides their cosmological significance the Pythagorean "numbers," had, as we have seen, fanciful symbolic interpretations, and apparently it was held that the various immaterial entities thus symbolized are to be found in the region of space which corresponds to the symbolic number in its cosmological interpretation; e. g., "opportunity" in that appropriated to the number 7. Aristotle then asks is the number 7, which they say is "opportunity," the same as that of which they say physical things are made, or different? E. g., is "opportunity" a figure made up of seven visible points? If "opportunity," "injustice," etc., are numbers, and bodies are also numbers, we must mean something very different by "number" in the two cases. Christ, in his second edition, retains μέν συμβαίνει and οὗτος, and, with Zeller, inserts τοῦτο before ἤδη in line 26. This gives us the sense: "and when they say as a proof of this that each of these is a number, and *that* just *this* multitude of magnitudes happens to be already constituted in this region, because," etc. I cannot understand the implied reasoning.

[1] "These things" appears now not to mean, as in the last sentence, opportunity, etc., but the extended figures and bodies previously referred to.

place, in the attempt to discover the causes of the entities of the actual world[1] they introduced the notion of a second class of entities equally numerous with them.[2] This is just as if one who wished to count certain things should fancy that while they remain fewer he will not succeed, but should first multiply them and then count. For the Ideas are pretty nearly as numerous as, or not fewer than, the things by inquiring into whose causes they advanced from actual objects to Ideas. For there is something synonymous corresponding to every group not only of substances but of all other things in which there is a One over the Many,[3] both in this world of actual things and in that of eternal things.

Again, none of the methods of argument by which we try to prove the existence of the Ideas

[1] τῶνδὲ τῶν ὄντων, "entities *here*" in the actual world perceptible by sense, as contrasted with things *there*, i. e., in the "intelligible world" of Plato's Ideas.

[2] The rest of the critique of Plato down to 991b 7, "of which we Platonists say there are not Ideas," appears again in *Metaphysics*, M, chs. 4, 5, in a form which is almost verbally identical with the present chapter, except that there Aristotle does not, as here, affect by the use of the pronoun of the first person plural to be speaking as a critic from within the Platonic circle itself. This repetition is one of many indications that the *Metaphysics* is in no sense a literary "work," prepared by its author for circulation.

[3] The "One over the Many" (ἓν ἐπὶ πολλῶν) is the single class-concept predicable of each severally of a plurality of individuals.

really establishes the conclusion. From some of them no necessary conclusion follows; from others, it follows that there would also be Ideas in cases where we do not believe in them. According to the arguments drawn from the sciences,[1] there will be Ideas of all things of which there are sciences. According to that based on the One over the Many,[2] there must be Ideas also of negatives, and according to that based on our ability to conceive of what has perished,[3] Ideas of

[1] This is the argument that, since there is exact and absolute truth, there must be a corresponding class of objects of knowledge, viz., the eternal, immutable Ideas. It occurs in Plato, e. g., at *Republic*, 478a; *Timæus*, 51. Aristotle objects that there are sciences of objects for which the Platonists themselves did not postulate corresponding Ideas, viz., negatives, relatives, artificial products. These limitations do not, however, occur in the Platonic dialogues. We read in the *Cratylus* (389) of an Idea of shuttle, in the *Republic* (597) of an Idea of bed—artificial products; in the *Phædo* and *Parmenides* of Ideas of equality and bigness—relations; in the *Parmenides* of an Idea of inequality—a negative.

[2] This appears to be what we might call the argument from the existence of a Limit, i. e., the inference of *Phædo*, 74 ff, that there must, e. g., be such a thing as *absolute* equality, which is never actually exhibited but only *suggested* as an ideal limit by the examples of *approximate* equality presented by sensuous perception. Aristotle's rather shallow objection would be most strikingly expressed by putting it in the form that since o is one of the most familiar instances of a limit, the argument from the existence of a limit requires that o should exist.

[3] The "argument from our ability to conceive what has perished" is best illustrated by Aristotle's own previous observation in ch. 6, that Plato held that the objects referred to in definitions cannot be sensible objects, since the definition is *always* equally true, but all sensible things are mutable.

perishable things; for there is a memory-image[1] of them. Besides, his most exact[2] arguments partly lead to Ideas of relatives, of which there is, according to us, no self-existing class, and partly bring the "third man"[3] into the argument. And, speaking generally, the arguments for the Ideas lead to the denial of things[4] whose reality we Platonists

[1] φάντασμα.

[2] These, according to Alexander, are the arguments which make the relation between the Idea and the corresponding class of sensible objects more definite by saying that the Idea is the *Original* (παράδειγμα) of which the sensible thing is a *copy* (ὁμοίωμα or μίμημα), i. e., the arguments in which the Idea appears as an Ideal Limit or Standard.

[3] The "third man" is the difficulty known in modern logic as the "indefinite regress." We learn from Alexander that it had been originally raised by the sophist, Polyxenus. Plato himself alludes to it in *Republic*, 597, and explicitly states it in *Parmenides*, 132, though without formally indicating his answer to it. It runs thus: If the likeness between Socrates, Plato, and other persons proves that they are all "copies" of a common archetype, the "Idea of Man," then the likeness between this Idea and Socrates must also prove that both Socrates and the Idea are "copies" of another common archetype, which will be a second and more ultimate Idea of Man; and the likeness between the first and second Ideas of Man proves the existence of a third Idea, which is *their* common archetype, and so on in *indefinitum*. (The real solution of the puzzle is that the relation between Socrates and "man" is not the same as the relation between Socrates and Plato. Socrates and Plato are both members of the class *men*; "man" is not a member of the class "men." Hence the argument of Polyxenus and Aristotle is a sophism, and the difficulty about the "regress" does not arise except in the case of those classes which can be members of themselves. On these classes, see Russell, *Principles of Mathematics*, I., ch. X., and Appendix B.)

[4] The "things" in question, Alexander explains, are the constituent elements of the Ideas themselves, the One and the Dyad of the

are even more concerned to maintain than that of the Ideas. For it follows from them that it is not the Dyad but number which is logically primary, that the relative is prior to the absolute, and all the other inconsistencies between the consequences which have been drawn from the theory of Ideas and its principles. Further, according to the conviction on which our Ideal theory is based, there will be Ideas not only of substances, but of much else (for there are common concepts not only in the case of substances but in other cases, and sciences not only of substances but of other entities, and there is a host of similar consequences). But according to rigid logic, and the

Great and Small. Aristotle contends that the theory of Ideas leads to consequences which are incompatible with the initial assumption as to these elements. E. g., if the Great and Small is one of the two constituents of every Idea, it must be a simpler notion presupposed in every Idea and thus logically prior to all the Ideas. Therefore it must, of course, be prior to the Idea of Number. But, since you can say, e. g., "The Great and Small are a *pair of* entities" or "are *two* entities," and two is *a* number, number should be the class, or universal, of which the Dyad is one instance, and it ought to follow that number is logically prior to what Plato regards as one of its simple constituents. (The reader will readily perceive that this, again, is a sophism, turning on the identification of the Indeterminate Dyad or "Variable" with the *number 2*. The repeated instances of this identification which occur both in this chapter and throughout book *M* afford a striking illustration of Aristotle's deficiency in exact mathematical thought.) He further goes on to object that Plato's theory makes the "relative" prior to the "absolute." This is because the fundamental concepts of that theory, "number" and "archetype," are relative terms. (Every number or archetype is a number or archetype *of* something.)

accepted theory of the Ideas, if things are related to the Ideas by "participation" there can be Ideas only of substances. For things do not "partake" of them *per accidens*; they only partake of each Idea in so far as it is not predicated of something else as a substitute. What I mean is, e. g., that if anything partakes of the Idea of "double" it also partakes of something eternal, but only *per accidens*, for it is an accident of the Idea of "double" to be eternal.[1] Hence the Ideas must be of substances.[2] But the same terms which denote substance *here*[3] denote it also *there*; or what else can be meant by saying that there is **991 a.** besides the actual things here something which is the unity corresponding to their multiplicity? And if the Ideas and the things which partake of

[1] The point is this: You can say, e. g., "a right-hand glove and a left-hand glove are *two* gloves"; thus in Platonic phrase, the gloves "partake of the Idea of" *two*. But though the Idea of *two*, like all Ideas, is eternal, you cannot say "these two gloves are eternal," for gloves, as we know, wear out. In the terminology of Aristotelian logic the relation of "participation," if it exists, must be between the sensible thing and the *substance* of the corresponding Idea, not between the thing and the *accidents* of the Idea.

[2] Reading with Bonitz in his Commentary, p. 114, and apparently with Alexander, οὐσίας in line 34 for MSS. οὐσία which Christ keeps The MSS. text gives the sense, "the Ideas must be substances," but *this* is throughout assumed by Aristotle as admitted.

[3] "Here" = among sensible things, "there" = among the Ideas, in the "intelligible" world, a mode of expression which became afterward technical with the Neoplatonists.

them are members of the same class, they will have something in common. For why should duality be one and the same thing in the case of the perishable pairs and that of the pairs which though many are eternal, and not equally so in the case of the Idea of duality and a particular pair of things?[1] But if they are not members of the same class, they can have nothing but their name in common, and it is much as if one called both Callias and a wooden image *men*, without reference to any community of character in them.[2]

---

[1] The many pairs of things which are eternal are, of course, the instances of couples which occur in pure Mathematics (e. g., pairs of conjugate diameters, pairs of asymptotes). The argument is our old friend, the "third man." "To be a couple," he contends, is predicable alike of the Idea of "two" and of a sensible couple. You can say: "The Idea of 'two' and this pair of gloves are *two couples*." Therefore, on Platonic principles, there must be a second more ultimate Idea of "two," in which both the first Idea of "two" and the gloves "participate." The sophistical character of the reasoning becomes obvious when we reflect that the Idea of "two" is *not* itself two things, but one thing. Do not confuse this Idea of "two" with the *Indeterminate* Dyad.

[2] At this point the parallel passage of book *M* (1079b 3) adds the following paragraph:

But if we assume that in general the universal concept coincides with the Idea (e. g., the qualification "plane figure" and the other constituents of the definition with the "Idea of the circle"), but that, in the case of the Idea, it must be further specified of *what* this Idea is the archetype, one has to consider whether this addition is not purely empty. To which constituent of the definition is it to be added? To "center," to "plane," or to all alike? For all the constituents of the essence are Ideas, e. g., "animal" and "biped." [I. e., in the definition of man as a two-footed animal. TR.] Besides, clearly it [i. e.,

Above all, it would be difficult to explain what the Ideas contribute to sensible things, whether to those which are eternal[1] or those which undergo generation and dissolution. For they are not the causes of any movement or change in them. But, once more, they are also of no assistance for the *knowledge* of other things (for the Ideas are not the substance of things; if they were, they would be *in* the things); nor do they contribute to their *Being*, since they are not *present in* the things which partake of them.[2] If they were, they might perhaps be thought to be causes in the sense in which an admixture of white is the cause that something is white. But this line of

the proposed extra qualification by which the Idea is to be distinguished from a mere universal generic concept, viz., that it is "the archetype of a class of sensible things." TR.] must itself be an entity, just as "plane" is an entity which must be present as a genus in all the species. [i. e., he argues that the same grounds which lead the Platonists to say that there is an Idea of "plane" of which circles, ellipses, and all the other plane figures "partake" would equally lead to the view that there is an Idea of "archetype" of which all the other Ideas "partake"—a fresh application of the "third man." TR.]

[1] i. e., the heavenly bodies, which, according to Aristotle, are ungenerated and incorruptible.

[2] This is the essence of Aristotle's most telling objection to the Platonic doctrine, viz., that Plato regarded the Ideas as "separable" from the sensible things which, nevertheless, depend on them for their Being. In modern terminology the point is, that Plato holds that what we mean to assert in a typical proposition of the form "X is a Y" (e. g., "Socrates is a man") is a *relation* between X (Socrates) and a *second* entity Y ("humanity," the "Idea of Man"). Aristotle regards this as an impossible analysis.

thought, which was first enunciated by Anaxagoras, and repeated later by Eudoxus and others, is easily refutable, for it is an easy task to collect many impossible consequences in opposition to such a doctrine.[1]

Once more, other things are not derived from the Ideas in any of the established senses of the term "derivation"; to call them "archetypes" and to say that other things "partake" of them is to employ empty words and poetical metaphors. For what is the agency which actually constructs things with the Idea as its model? A thing may both be and become like something else without being imitated from it. Thus whether Socrates exists or not, there may equally be some one like Socrates, and it is clear that the case would not be altered even if Socrates were eternal. Also, there will be many archetypes, and consequently many Ideas, for the same thing; e. g., "animal" and "biped" will be archetypes in the case of man, as well as the "Idea of Man." Further, the Ideas

---

[1] Plato's friend, Eudoxus of Cnidus, the astronomer, had attempted to meet the objection just mentioned by saying that things are a "mixture" in which the Idea is one ingredient. Aristotle regards this as analogous to the doctrine of Anaxagoras, according to which every thing contains some degree of all the contrasted qualities of matter, but exhibits to our senses only those of which it has most. The "consequences" are, no doubt, of the same kind as those urged in ch. 8, against Anaxagoras. Alexander says that Aristotle had developed them more at length in his lost work, "On Ideas."

will be archetypes not only of sensible things, but of Ideas themselves, e. g., the genus will be the archetype of the species contained in it. So one and the same thing will be both archetype and copy.[1] Besides, it may surely be regarded as **991 b.** an impossibility that the substance of a thing and the thing of which it is the substance should be separated. So, how can the Ideas, if they are the substances of things, be separate from them?

In the *Phædo*[2] we are told that the Ideas are causes both of Being and of Becoming. And yet, even if the Ideas exist, the things which partake of them do not come into being unless there is something to set the process in motion; and many other things come into being, e. g., a house, a ring, of which we Platonists say there are not Ideas. Hence, clearly, it is possible for other things as well both to exist and come into being through

[1] He means that if from 'Socrates is a man" you can infer the existence of an "Idea of Man" of which Socrates "partakes," you ought equally from "Man is an animal" to infer an "Idea of Animal" of which "the Idea of Man" partakes.

[2] Phædo, 100d: "When I am told that anything is beautiful because it has a goodly colour or shape, or anything else of the kind, I pay no attention to such talk, for it only confuses me. I cling simply, plainly, perhaps foolishly, to my own inner conviction that nothing makes a thing beautiful but the presence, or communication, whatever its nature may be, of that Ideal Beauty. Without any further assertion as to the nature of this relation, I assert merely that it is through Beauty that all beautiful things are beautiful."

the agency of causes of the same kind as those of the objects just referred to.[1]

Further, if the Ideas are *numbers*, how can they be causes? Perhaps, because things are a second set of numbers; e. g., this number is Man, that Socrates, that again Callias. But why, then, are the first set of numbers considered the *causes* of the others? For it will make no difference that the one are eternal and the others not. But if the explanation is that things *here* are *ratios* between numbers — e. g., a musical concord — plainly, there is some one thing *of* which they are ratios. Now, if there is such a thing, viz., matter, manifestly the numbers themselves must be ratios of one thing to a second. I mean that, e. g., if Callias is a numerical ratio of fire, earth, water, and air, the Idea, too, must be a number of some other things which are its substrate, and the "Ideal Man," whether a number or not, still will be a numerical ratio *of* certain things, and not simply

---

[1] The argument has two branches. (1) The mere existence of the Idea is not enough to guarantee that of a corresponding group of sensible things. (E. g., the existence of an "Idea of Man" does not secure the existence of Socrates. Socrates must have had parents, and his existence depends on certain *acts* of those parents.) (2) And artificial products, on the other hand, certainly come into being. Yet the Platonists, according to Aristotle, say that there are no Ideas of such products. Why then, if houses and rings can come into being, though there are no Ideas of them, may the same not be true of everything else?

a number, nor does it follow on these grounds that he will be a number.[1]

Again, one number can be composed of many other numbers, but how can one Idea be formed of many Ideas? If you say it is not composed of the numbers themselves, but of the units contained in them, e. g., those of the number 10,000, what is the relation between these units? If they are all homogeneous, many paradoxical consequences must follow; if they are not homogeneous, neither those of the same number with one another nor all with all, what can make the difference between them, seeing that they have no qualities?[2] Such thinking is neither rational nor consistent.

[1] The paragraph develops further the contention that numbers are *relative* terms. The argument is as follows: He suggests that Plato may have reconciled the assertions that the Ideas are Numbers and that they are the causes of things by the view that a sensible thing (e. g., the organism of Callias) is a combination of certain materials in accordance with a definite numerical law. This law would be, in Aristotelian phrase, the "form" or "formal" *cause* of the thing in question. Only, in that case, the thing in question (the body of Callias) is not merely a numerical law, but a law of the combination of certain specific material. Consequently, if the sensible thing (the body of Callias) is a copy of a certain archetype (the "Idea of Man"), this archetype also must contain something corresponding to the material factor in the thing, and thus even on Plato's own principles, the Idea will not be merely a "number" but a numerical law of the combination *of* certain material. There seems to be an allusion to the formation of the human organism out of materials which are definite compounds of the four "elements," as described in the *Timæus*.

[2] Aristotle's point is, that any two numbers can be added together and their sum will be a third number of the same kind. But Ideas,

Again, it becomes necessary to construct a second kind of number which is the object of Arithmetic and all the studies which have been called "intermediate." How or out of what principles can this be constructed? And on what grounds must it be regarded as "intermediate" between things *here* and the ideal numbers?[1] Again, each of the units in the Dyad[2] must be or class-concepts, he thinks, cannot be added. If they are numbers, they must be numbers composed of units which, unlike those of Arithmetic, are not all of the same kind, and therefore cannot always be added so as to produce a resultant of the same kind as the factors. He thinks that you may then suppose either that each of the units which compose one and the same "Ideal number" may be of the same kind as all the other units of *that* number, but different in kind from any of the units of a different "Ideal number," or that even the units of one and the same "Ideal number" may be all different in kind from one another, the former being the more natural hypothesis. The two forms of the supposition, which are here curtly dismissed, are discussed at length in *M*, ch. 7, 8, 1081a 1-1083a 20. The reader will see that Aristotle's philosophy of number is doubly defective, since (1) he has no conception of the dependence of arithmetical addition on the more fundamental process of *logical* addition (for which see Russell, *Principles of Mathematics*, I., ch. XII.); (2) and he has, also, no conception of any class of numbers except the integers. (On this point, see Milhaud, *Les Philosophes-Géomètres de la Grèce*, pp. 359-365, who well asks by what addition of integers Aristotle could have obtained such numbers as $\sqrt{2}$, $\sqrt{3}$.)

[1] For a detailed attack on the conception of mathematical objects as "intermediate" between Ideas and sensible things, see *M*, ch. 2, p. 1076a 37 ff.

[2] I. e., the Indeterminate Dyad of the Great and Small. The argument is, that since this is a dyad or "pair," it must consist of two members; whence, then, are these derived? (You must not say that they are repetitions of the other element, the One, because in the Platonic

derived from a prior Dyad; but this is impossible. Again, why is a number of units when formed into a collection one thing?[1] Again, in addition to all this, if the units differ, the Platonists have followed the example of those who maintain four or two elements. Each of these thinkers gives the name of *element* not to their common substrate, e. g., body — but to fire and earth, whether they have a common substrate, viz., body, or not. But the One is in fact spoken of as if it were as homogeneous as fire or water. But if it is homogeneous in this sense, the numbers

992 a.

system the "Great and Small" is regarded as being logically no less ultimate and elementary than the One.) Here, again, we have, as Bonitz observes, an unfair identification of the "Indeterminate Dyad" with the *number* 2. It is only the latter, not the former, which can be said to consist of two units. And even in the case of the latter such an expression is a loose and inaccurate way of saying that 2 is the number determined by the addition of 1 to 1, or the number of the terms of a class formed by uniting in one class the terms of the classes *a* and *b*, when *a* and *b* each have only one term and their terms are not identical.

[1] i. e., each Idea is one thing or unit, an entity corresponding to one determinate class or type. How then, can it also be a *number,* which is a collection of units? Cf. *H,* 1044a 2, where the same complaint is made that the Platonists cannot explain what it is that makes a number *one* thing, and *M,* 1082a 15, where he asks, "how can the number 2 be an entity distinct from its two units?" This and many other passages of *M* show how very literally and naïvely Aristotle conceives of integers as formed by addition. What he does not see is, that "addition is not primarily a method of forming numbers, but of forming classes or collections. If we add *B* to *A* we do not obtain the number 2, but we obtain *A* and *B,* which is a collection of two terms, or a couple." (Russell, *op. cit.* p. 135.)

cannot be substances; rather, it is manifest that if there is a self-existing One and this One is a first principle, "one" is an equivocal term.[1] In any other case it is an impossibility.

When we[2] wish to refer our substances to their principles we derive length from the Short and Long, a special case of the Small and Great, the plane from the Broad and Narrow, body from the High and Low. Yet, how can the line be contained in the plane, or the line and plane in the solid? The Broad and Narrow is a different genus from the High and Low. So, just as numbers are not contained in these classes, because the Many and Few is a different class from them, clearly no other of the higher genera will be contained in the lower.[3] Nor, again, is the Broad

[1] i. e., the kind of number meant by the Platonists when they speak of their Ideas as numbers must be something quite different from what the arithmetician means by number.

[2] i. e., "we Platonists."

[3] The argument is aimed at the Platonic application of the principles of the One and the Great and Small to define geometrical extension in one, two, three dimensions. The point is, that whereas, according to Aristotle, a solid contains surfaces, a surface lines, and a line points, this could not be the case on the Platonic principles, according to which each of the three dimensions consists of magnitudes of a different *kind*. (Cf. *M*, 9, 1085a 7-31.) Hence, he holds, a Platonist ought not to be able to define a plane in terms of the definition of a straight line, nor a solid in terms of the definition of a plane, or vice versa. Now, Aristotle holds that you can do the latter. A plane is, e. g., the *boundary* of a solid; a straight line is the *boundary* of a plane (as we should say, the intersection of two planes). This is what he

the genus of which the High is a species, for if it were so, body would be a kind of plane.

Again, how will it be possible for *points* to "be in" figures? Plato, in fact, rejected this class of entities as a mere fiction of the geometers. He used to speak of them as the "beginning of the line," for which he often employed the expression "indivisible line." But even these lines must have a limit, so that the same argument which proves the existence of the line proves, also, that of the point.[1]

means by planes being "in" solids, and lines "in" planes. He does not, of course, mean that, as the Pythagoreans had thought, a solid is actu-ally made up of superposed laminæ, or a plane of juxtaposed strips. The argument is, however, fallacious; since, e. g., a plane may quite well be, as the Platonists held, a different kind of magnitude from a straight line and yet be definable in terms of the definition of a straight line.   Aristotle has, in fact, been led astray by his inadequate theory of definition as being exclusively by genus and difference.   "Higher" genera means, of course, those which require for their conception a higher degree of abstraction and analysis.

[1] Aristotle is referring to a view, known from the commentators to have been held by Xenocrates, and here attributed by him to Plato himself, that there are really no such entities as points, what we call a point being, in fact, not a magnitude but the "starting point" ($\dot{\alpha}\rho\chi\dot{\eta}$) or "beginning" of a magnitude, viz., of the line.   There is no trace of this doctrine in the dialogues of Plato, and the imperfect tense ($\dot{\epsilon}\varkappa\dot{\alpha}\lambda\epsilon\iota$) shows that Aristotle is referring not to any Platonic passage, but to verbal statements made by Plato in his lectures.   Since the view in question was adopted by Xenocrates, the actual president of the Academy during Aristotle's activity in Athens as a teacher, it is natural that he should have treated it to special criticism; among the extant works ascribed to him there is, in fact, a special tract, "On

To speak generally, though it is the business of wisdom to discover the cause of visible things, we have neglectedth at task (for we have nothing to say about the cause by which change is initiated), but in the fancy that we are describing their substance we assert the existence of a second class of substances, though our explanation of the way in which they are substances *of* the former set is empty verbiage, for "participation," as I have said, is nothing at all. Nor do the Ideas stand in any connection with the kind of cause which we observe in the practical[1] sciences, the cause *for the sake of* which all Mind and all Nature act, and which we have included among our first principles. Mathematics has been termed by our present-day thinkers into the whole of Philosophy, in

Indivisible Lines." Plato's difficulty, no doubt, was that the point has *no* dimensions; it is a *zero* magnitude. The error of refusing to admit the point, or zero dimension, is exactly analogous to the universal error of Greek arithmeticians in regarding 1, not 0, as the first of the integers. Though, since the definition of a point, often cited by Aristotle as a "unit having position," seems to come from Pythagorean and Platonic sources (Cf. *M*, 8, 1084b 26, 33), it seems possible that Aristotle (and Xenocrates?) may have misunderstood what Plato meant by calling the point an "indivisible line," as is maintained by Milhaud, *op. cit.* p. 341-2. The reader will note that, though Aristotle's conclusion that Geometry requires the point is sound, his argument is a *petitio principii*, since it *assumes* the existence of the limit.

[1] I follow Zeller in making the necessary addition of $\pi o \iota \eta \tau \iota \kappa \acute{a}s$ before $\grave{\epsilon}\pi\iota\sigma\tau\acute{\eta}\mu as$ in line 29.

spite of their declaration that it ought to be studied for the sake of something further.[1]   **992 b.**

Besides, we may fairly regard the entity which
they assume as matter as being more properly of a
mathematical kind, and as being rather a predicate and a specific difference of substance and
matter than identical with matter itself. I mean
the Great and the Small; just as the physicists,
when speaking of rarity and density, say that
these are the primary specific differences of the
material substrate, for they are a kind of excess
and defect. And as to motion, if these elements[2]
are to constitute motion, plainly the ideas will
be in motion;[3] if they are not to constitute it,
whence has it come? Thus the whole study of
physical Nature is abolished. And even the
proof, which is fancied to be so easy, that all things
are one, does not follow. Their method of
"exposition,"[4] even if one grants all their assump-

[1] The reference is specially to the place assigned to Mathematics
as a propædeutic to the study of the Ideas in *Republic*, VII., particularly
to 531d: "All these are mere preludes to the hymn which has to be
learned. For you surely do not consider those who are proficients in
them as dialecticians."

[2] viz., the Great and Small.

[3] Because the Great and Small is a constituent of every Idea.
That the Ideas should "be in motion" is impossible, on Platonic principles, because one chief characteristic of them is their immutability.

[4] The method here and elsewhere called by Aristotle "exposition" (ἔκθεσις) is the familiar Platonic procedure of inferring from

tions, does not prove that all things are one, but only that there *is* a self-existing One, and does not even prove this unless it is granted that the universal is a genus; but in some cases that is impossible. And as for the objects they consider logically posterior to the numbers, viz., lines and planes and solids, no rational grounds can be produced to show how they exist or can exist, nor what character they possess. They cannot be Ideas (for they are not numbers), nor the "intermediate" class of objects (for these are mathematical figures), nor yet can they be identical with perishable things. Manifestly, we have here, again, a fresh and a fourth class of objects.[1]

In general, it is impossible to discover the ele-

the existence of many individual things possessing some common predicate the existence of a *single* supersensible entity, the Idea, which is their common archetype. He objects (1) that the argument, in any case, does not prove that all the individual things *are* one thing, but only that, beside them, there is *one* ideal archetype of which they are all copies; (2) it does not even prove this unless the common predicate is the name of a "real kind" or genus. This is a corollary from his previous conclusion that if there are Ideas they can only be Ideas of substances.

[1] The point is this: The Platonists hold that the many lines, planes, solids, of Geometry are *copies* of certain single archetypal entities—*the* line, *the* plane, *the* solid. These are the "objects posterior to the "Numbers" here spoken of. But what *are* these objects? Not Ideas (since they are not numbers, and every Idea is a number); not geometrical figures (since geometrical figures are copies of *them*); not physical things, since they are immutable. Thus they must be a fourth class of objects, not provided for in the Platonic classification of

ments of existing things if one does not first distinguish the different "senses of existence," especially
when the inquiry is directed towards the problem
of what elements existing things are composed.
For one certainly cannot discover what are the
elements of which activity or passivity or straight-
ness is composed. If the problem is soluble at
all, it is only soluble in the case of substances.[1]
So it is an error to ask after, or to think one has
found, the elements of everything. How, indeed,

objects into Ideas, mathematical objects, and sensible things. This
argument is further developed in great detail in ch. 2, of book
M, given in appendix D.

[1] He concludes his polemic by an attack on the general theory
of the nature of science which is tacitly implied in the Platonic doctrine, viz., that the objects of all the sciences are composed of the
same constituent elements. He has already explained that Plato
thought that the elements of the Ideas are the elements of everything.
It follows that there is ultimately only one science, viz., Dialectic,
which, as we learn from *Republic*, VI., 511, cognizes the ultimate axioms
from which *all* scientific truth can be deduced. Aristotle holds that
there is no such supreme science of first principles; every science has
its own special subject-matter, and consequently its own special axioms
(*Analytica Posteriora*, I., 76a 16). In this passage he urges two objections to the Platonic view. (1) Analysis into constituent elements is only
possible in the case of substances. In a substance you have always
the two constituent logical elements of *matter* and *form* (which appear
in its definition as *genus* and *difference*), but these elements cannot
be found in a quality, an action, or a state. Cf. *H*. 1044b 8:
"Things which exist in nature, but are not substances, have no matter, but their substrate is their substance. E. g., what is the cause of
an *eclipse?* What is its matter? There is none, but the *moon* is the
thing affected." He means, then, that Plato thinks that in the end
all objects of knowledge are *made of* the same ingredients, and

could one possibly learn the elements of everything? For it is clear that one could not possibly
have been in previous possession of any information at all. Just as he who is learning geometry
may very well have previous knowledge about
other things, but has no previous acquaintance
with the truths which belong to that science, and
which he is about to learn, so it is in all other
cases. So, if there is, as some assert, a universal
science of everything, he who learns it must have
no previous acquaintance with anything. And
yet all learning is effected through previous
acquaintance with some or all of the matters con-

therefore there is only one science of them all; but Aristotle says
there is no sense in asking what qualities or activities are *made* of.
(2) The second objection depends on the principle that all learning
of anything depends on and requires previous knowledge. (See
Appendix A.) To learn the truth by *demonstration*, you must previously know the *premises* of the proof; to learn it from a *definition*,
you must know the meaning of the *terms* employed; to learn it
by *induction*, i. e., comparison of instances, you must previously
be acquainted with the individual instances. Hence if all truths constituted a single science, before learning that science you would know
no truths at all, and therefore the process of learning itself would be
impossible. To meet the retort which a Platonist, who held with
Plato that all knowledge is really recollection, would be sure to make,
viz., that the knowledge of the ultimate axioms is "innate," and not
acquired at all (Cf. Plato, *Meno*, 81c, etc.), he argues that if we had
such innate cognitions we could not be unconscious of having them —
the same argument afterward employed by Locke.

As an argument against the doctrine of an all-embracing science
the reasoning seems a pure *petitio principii*, since it merely goes to
prove the necessity of some self-evident truths.

cerned. This is true both of learning from demonstration and of learning from definitions. The parts which compose the definition must be previously known and familiar. The same is true, also, of learning from induction. But if it **993 a.** be suggested that this knowledge is really innate, it is surely a mystery how we can possess the most excellent of sciences and yet be unconscious of the fact. Besides, how are we to *recognize* what existence consists of? How can the result be *established?*[1] There is a difficulty implied here, since the same doubt might be suggested as about certain syllables. Some say that the syllable ZA consists of Σ, Δ, and Α, others that it is a distinct sound, different from those already familiar. Besides, how could one become acquainted with the objects of sense-perception, without possessing the corresponding form of sense-perception? Yet, this ought to be possible if all things

[1] i. e., even when you have analysed everything back into its simple elements, how are you to recognize the fact that they *are* simple and that the analysis cannot be carried any further?—an objection which, one might think, is as much or as little applicable to Aristotle's own analysis of a thing into matter and form as to Plato's analysis of everything into the One and the Great and the Small. The illustration about the analysis of a syllable into its simple constituent sounds is from Plato, *Theaetetus*, 203a, where, however, the application of it is rather different. Aristotle's point is, that while some grammarians regard the sound of the Greek letter Z (which appears to have been equivalent to our *ds*) as simple, others hold that it can be analysed further into the two sounds of Σ and Δ.

are composed of the same constituent elements,[1] as composite articulate sounds are composed of their own special elements.[2]

CHAPTER X.

It is clear, then, even from the preceding review, that all philosophers seem to be investigating the forms of cause enumerated in our discourses on Physics, and that we can specify no further form of cause beside these. But their treatment of them was obscure, and though in one sense all the causes had been previously recognized, in another sense this had not been done at all. For at first, and in its beginnings, owing to its youth, the earliest philosophy resembled in its utterances on all topics the lisping speech of an infant. Thus even Empedocles says that the existence of *bone* depends on a ratio,[3] but this ratio is, in fact, the

---

[1] i. e., if, for instance, a visible object, such as a shade or color, is ultimately constituted by a combination of purely logical categories, like the One and the Great and Small (as must be the case if the "elements of the Ideas are the elements of all things"), a Platon'c philosopher, even though blind from birth, ought to be able to have "pure anticipated cognitions" of all the colors of the spectrum.

[2] This clause is plausibly regarded by Christ as a misplaced gloss on the words of the sentence: "Some say that the syllable——— Σ, Δ, and Δ," above.

[3] λόγος. The reference is to Empedocles, 199ff, where bone is said to consist of fixed proportions of the elementary bodies. The

essential nature or *essence*[1] of the object. But it follows with equal necessity that there must also be a ratio for flesh, and every other individual thing, or for none at all. This, then, and not the matter, of which Empedocles speaks, viz., fire, and earth and water and air, will be the true ground of the existence of flesh and bone and everything else. If another had explained this he would have had no alternative but to admit it, but he did not express it clearly himself. These and similar points, then, have been explained above, but we may now return to the consideration of the difficulties which might be raised about these same topics. Perhaps a study of them may pave the way for an answer to our subsequent difficulties.

point is, simply, that Empedocles is recognizing that what a thing is depends primarily on its *form* or *formal cause*, or, as we should say, the *law* of its composition, and not merely on the nature of the *stuff* of which it is made.

[1] τὸ τί ἦν εἶναι καὶ ἡ οὐσία.

APPENDIX.

APPENDIX.

___

A.

On the Cognition of Universal Axioms, as a product of Experience. (Cf. Met., *A*, 1, 980a 27-b29, 9, 992b 25ff.) *Analytica Posteriora*, 2, 71a 1-16.

All instruction and all processes of intellectual[1] learning depend upon the presence of antecedent cognitions. This will become manifest if we consider the various cases *seriatim.*[2] The mathematical sciences and every one of the other arts are acquired in this manner. The same is true of logic, both syllogistic and inductive; in both cases the instruction is derived from antecedent cognitions. In the former premises are assumed, with the implication that their sense is understood; in the latter a universal is established by the manifest truth of the individual instances.

[1] The qualifying epithet is intended to exclude cognition through immediate sense-perception on the one hand and the immediate intuition of ultimate axioms on the other.

[2] The argument which follows is a typical Aristotelian "inductive syllogism," i e., a demonstration that a predicate *a* belongs universally to a genus *A* by showing that it belongs separately to each of the subordinate species into which *A* can be exhaustively subdivided. Mathematical and scientific reasoning, λόγοι or philosophic science not aided by sensuous diagrams, rhetorical reasoning, are treated as the three species of the genus "inferential knowledge."

Rhetorical arguments, again, produce conviction in the same way, either by means of examples (and this is induction) or by means of *enthymemes*[1] (and this is syllogism). The antecedent cognition necessary may be of two kinds. In some cases we require previous recognition of the truth of a statement, in others, previous understanding of the sense of a term; in others again, both are needed. E. g., in the case of the proposition that "every proposition can either be truly affirmed or truly denied"[2] we have to presuppose the truth of a statement; in the case of "triangle," the meaning of a term; in the case of "the number 1," both the meaning of the term and the existence of the thing denoted.[2]

Analytica Posteriora, II., 19, 99b 20–100b 17.

We have already said that it is impossible to have scientific knowledge as the result of demonstration without cognition of the ultimate axiomatic principles.[3] But a difficulty might be raised as to the cognition of these axioms themselves. Is it of the same kind as the cognition of demonstrated truth. Tr.], or of a different kind? Are both the objects of science, or is the one the object of science, the other of a different form of cognition? Also, does the cognition of axioms make its appearance in consciousness, having previously been absent, or is it unconsciously present

[1] "Enthymemes" not in the modern but in the Aristotelian sense of "inference from likelihood or presumptive evidence."

[2] This is meant for a formulation of the law of Excluded Middle.

[3] τάς πρώτας ἀρχὰς τὰς ἀμέσους, "first and *immediate* principles," i. e., axioms incapable of being syllogistically deduced, through a middle term, from any more general and ultimate principles.

from the first?[1] It is certainly strange if we possess it from
the first. For it follows that we possess cognitions which
are more accurate than demonstration, and yet are unconscious of the fact. Yet, if we do not at first possess them
but afterward acquire them, how come we to apprehend
and learn them, except on a basis of antecedent cognition?
For that, as was said in speaking of demonstrative proof,
is impossible. It is plain, then, that we can neither possess
them from the first nor could they appear in consciousness
if we were ignorant of them and had no disposition to
acquire them. One is thus driven to conclude that we have
a certain faculty of acquiring them, but not of such a kind
as to rank higher than demonstrated truth in respect of
accuracy.[2] Now, such a faculty is obviously present in all
animals. They have a congenital faculty of discrimination,
which is called sense-perception. On the occurrence of
sensation there supervenes in some animals retention of
the sense-percept, in others not. Where it does not occur
universally, or with respect to certain sensations, the animal
has no cognition beyond the sensation; where it does occur

---

[1] The two alternatives, both of which he finds unsatisfactory,
are pure Empiricism and the Platonic doctrine of recollection, which
he interprets as a theory of "innate ideas." He proceeds to mediate
between these alternatives much as Leibniz did between the doctrines
of Locke and Descartes.

[2] $\tau o \acute{v} \tau \omega \nu$, in line 33, I take to mean $\tau \tilde{\omega} \nu \ \dot{\alpha} \pi o \delta \epsilon \iota \xi \acute{\epsilon} \omega \nu$.
The meaning of the "accuracy" or "exactness" here spoken of
will be perceived by reference to *Analytica Post.*, I., 27, 87a 33,
where we are told that a science which deals with universal relations
in abstraction is more "exact" than one which considers their application to a special subject-matter (e. g., Arithmetic than Harmonics),
and a science which makes few initial postulates than one which
makes more (e. g., Arithmetic than Geometry).

the animal can, after sensation is over, preserve some result of it in consciousness. When this process is frequently repeated a further distinction makes its appearance; in some animals such retention leads to rational cognition, in others not. Thus, as I say, sense-perception gives rise to memory, and repeated memories of the same object to experience; for the numerically many memories form a single experience. And experience, i. e., any establishment in consciousness of a universal, or one over and above the many, which is a point of identity present in them all,[1] leads to the principles of Art and Science; of Art if it is concerned with Production, of Science if it is concerned with Being.

These axiomatic cognitions thus are neither there from the first in a determinate form nor yet are they derived from other cognitions of a higher type,[2] but from sense-perception. The process is like what occurs in battle after a rout, when first one man makes a stand, and then a second and a third follow his example, and so at last order is established. The constitution of consciousness is such as to permit of this process.[3]

Let me repeat an explanation which has already been

---

[1] This clause is added to show that by the "one over and above the many" he means merely a subjective "general concept," not a Platonic Idea.

[2] γνωστικώτερων "naturally more knowable," i. e., logically simpler and therefore more ultimate.

[3] The point of the comparison lies in the fact that in the rally order and discipline come to be spontaneously re-established without the direct issuing of instructions to that effect by a superior. So, owing to the implicit generalising character of all cognition, axioms come spontaneously to be recognized in consequence of our perception of their validity in special applications, without any process of conscious formal deduction.

given, though without due precision. When a conviction has been established about any class of objects which are indistinguishable in kind, we have the earliest universal in consciousness; (for in fact, though the object perceived is an individual thing, sense perception is of the universal; e. g., of *man*, not of the man Callias). Generalisations are then established among these classes, and so we proceed, until we come to the establishment of the unanalysable universals. E. g., we pass from generalisations about "such and such a species of animal" to generalisations about "animal," and treat that concept in the same way. For even sense-perception in this way gives rise to universal cognitions.[1]

[1] Translation of the highly condensed expressions of this paragraph necessarily involves some amount of interpretative paraphrase, but I have endeavoured to keep as closely as possible to the actual words of the text. The key to its meaning is given by the parenthetical remark about the implicit universality of sense-perception. The spontaneous inductive process which leads from the simplest generalisations about the more obvious classes of sensible objects, through axiomata media—to use Bacon's familiar phrase— to the most universal of axioms, which are quite incapable of adequate representation by sensible illustrations, depends for its possibility upon the principle that though the *object* cognized in sense-perception itself is always a particular individual (the man Callias), the *content* of the perception, that which is cognized *about* the object, is always a universal, or complex of universals. The use of the expression ἀμερῆ "indivisibles" (rendered in the text "unanalysable") for the axioms of highest generality is, I suppose, explained by the fact that in Aristotle's theory of definition by genus and difference, the genus appears as a "part" of the intension of the species. (*Metaphysics*, Δ 25, 1023b 24: "Hence the genus is also called a part of the species, though in another sense the species is part of the genus.") Thus an "unanalysable" genus is one which cannot be regarded as a species of a higher class, an indefinable summum genus or highest universal.

Thus it is clear that we need to apprehend ultimate axioms by a process of *induction*.[1] And since of the intellectual conditions by which we perceive truth some are always truthful, while others admit of error (e. g., Opinion and Computation, whereas Science and Rational Intuition are always truthful); since, further, Rational Intuition[2] is the only type of cognition which is more exact than Science, while the principles of demonstration are "more knowable"[3] than the results of demonstration, and all Science involves inference, the cognition of axiomatic principles cannot be Science. Hence, since the only form of cognition which can have a higher truth than Science is Rational Intuition, it must be by Rational Intuition that axiomatic principles are cognized. This result follows, also, from the consideration that since the principles of demonstration are not themselves demonstration, those of Science cannot be themselves Science. So, if we have no type of true cognition except Science, Rational Intuition must be the principle from which Science starts.[4]

Ethica Nicomachea, vi.-xi., 1143a 35—b5.

[1] Induction, that is, in the Socratic sense; i. e., the general principle of the axiom is made clear to us in consequence of our previous recognition of its validity in particular classes of instances.

[2] νοῦς, "Mind;" i. e., a cognition which is at once rational and universal, and also like sense-perception at the other end of the series, immediate See the passage from the *Ethics*, which immediately follows.

[3] i. e., "naturally, in the logical order of concatenation of truths, more knowable;" that is, are simpler and more ultimate universal truths.

[4] Aristotle's view is thus twofold. The process by which the individual mind, as a fact in its psychological history, comes by the apprehension of the axioms is one of generalising induction from

It is Rational Intuition which apprehends the ultimates in both directions. For both the first and the last terms of our reasoning are apprehended by Rational Intuition, not by discursive reasoning. In demonstrations this intuition is of the primary and immutable principles, in the study of questions of conduct it is of contingent ultimate facts and minor premises, for these are the starting-point of purposive action, since its universal rules are based on particular cases. Of these cases, then, we must have an immediate perception, and that is Rational Intuition.

B.

The Four Senses of Cause.

Aristotle, *Metaphysics*, $\varDelta$ 2, 1013a24—b28. = *Physics* $\varPi$3, 194b 23-195a 26.

A *cause* signifies in one of its meanings that *out of which* anything is formed and which continues to exist in it; e. g., the bronze of the statue, the silver of the goblet, and the universal classes of these materials; in another meaning

---

examples. We are individually *led up* to the recognition of the principle by being familiarised with *examples* of its truth in concrete cases. But the "induction" in no sense *proves* the axiom; it merely calls attention to it. (Cf. 91b 33. "He who produces an example does not *prove* the conclusion, though he does *point out* something.)" The axiom is, in fact, neither proved nor provable. When the requisite illustrations have been produced, you simply have directly to *see* what the implied principle is, and, if you do not see it, no proof can make you see. Aristotle's view thus turns out to be simply the Platonic doctrine of "innate ideas" *minus* its imaginative psychological background of pre-existence. Whether the removal of this background is an improvement is a point on which opinions may possibly differ. The ultimate germ of the whole theory is the treatment of association as a source of suggestion in *Phædo*, p. 73 ff.

it signifies the *form* and the archetype,[1] i. e., the formula expressive of the essential nature[2] and its universal classes. E. g., that of the octave is the ratio 2:1, and universally number and the constituent parts of the definitory formula are causes of this kind. It signifies also the *first source of change or of rest*, e. g., the giver of advice is the cause of its consequences, the father of his offspring, and universally the agent of the act, the producer of change of the change produced. Also, the term is used in the sense of the *end*, i. e., the purpose for the sake of which anything is done; e. g., health is the cause, in this sense, of walking. For why does the man take walks? We answer, "in order to keep in health," and when we have said this we believe ourselves to have assigned the cause of his action. This applies also to what occurs under the agency of another in the process of attaining the end; e. g., in the case of health, the lowering treatment, the purgation, the physician's drugs and implements; they are all there for the sake of the end, though there is this difference among them that some of them are implements, others their effects. These, then, are the principal different senses of the term "cause." It follows that since the term is an equivocal one, there may be many causes of the same effect, and that not merely in an accidental sense. Thus, e. g., both the sculptor's art and the bronze are causes of the statue, and that not in respect of some further characteristic but in its character of a statue. But they are not its causes in the same sense of the term; the one is its cause in the sense of its material, the other in the sense of the source of movement. Things may also be reciprocally causes of each other; for instance, exertion

---

[1] παράδειγμα.

[2] τὸ τί ἦν εἶναι.

of good bodily condition, and this of exertion, but not in the same sense; the one is cause in the sense of end, the other in the sense of the source of motion.

Further, the same thing may in some cases be the cause of opposite results. When a thing, by its presence, is the cause of a given result, we sometimes regard it as being, by its absence, the cause of the opposite result. Thus the cause of a vessel's capsizing is said to be the absence of the captain, whose presence was the cause of her previous safety. And here both the presence and its negation are causes in the sense of sources of motion.

All the senses of cause which have now been enumerated fall into four most obvious classes. Letters of the alphabet are causes of syllables, raw materials are causes of manufactured products, fire, earth, and the like of bodies, the parts of the whole, the premises of the conclusion, in the sense that they are the factors from which they are formed. Of such factors, some are of the character of the substrate, e. g., the parts, others of that of the essential nature,[1] e. g., the totality, the synthesis of parts, the form.[2] The seed, the physician, the giver of advice, and universally the agent, are all instances of the source of change or quiescence. Other examples are instances of the end or good to which something else is relative. For that for the sake of which something takes place claims to be the best state and the end of something else. (We need not raise the question

[1] τὸ τί ἦν εἶναι.

[2] The structure of the Greek sentence is awkward, since it opens at "letters of the alphabet," as if reference were going to be made to the material "factor," or substrate, only, and is then unexpectedly enlarged so as to include the "form" and "essential nature" under the general rubric of "factors from which things are formed."

whether it ought to be called the real good or the apparent good.)[1]

[1] Aristotle's account of the Four Causes may be most readily understood by bearing in mind the etymological connection of the word αἴτιον αἰτία, "cause," with the adjective αἴτιος, "responsible for," "accountable for." The αἴτιον of any state of things is that to which, in the English vernacular idiom, the state of things in question can be "blamed." Now, when we ask, "what is responsible for the fact that such and such a state of things now exists, there are four obvious partial answers to be given, corresponding to the four Aristotelian senses of "cause." We may mention (1) the factors out of which the thing has been constructed — the *matter* or *material cause* of the thing; (2) the law according to which those factors have been combined — the *form* or *formal* cause; (3) the agent with whose initiating impulse the process of combination or development began — the *source of motion* or *efficient* cause, (4) the conscious and deliberate, or instinctive and subconscious purpose which the process of development has realized — the *end* or *final* cause. Had any one of these four been different, the resultant state of things would also have been in some degree different. Hence they all are "responsible for" the result, that is, are its *causes*. The most obvious illustrations, given as such by Aristotle, are to be found in the case of artificial products of human skill, such as, e. g., a statue. The statue would not be what it is if (a) its *matter* had been different, e. g., if the sculptor had used bronze or wood instead of marble; a (b) if its *form* had been different, e. g., if he had hewed the marble into the lineaments of Hercules instead of Apollo; (c) or if the material had been subjected to a different series of *movements* on the part of the artificer, e. g., if he had cut it into blocks for pediments, or (4) if he had not *aimed* at producing this result but some other; e. g., if he or his patron had wanted an obelisk, and not a statue. It seems clear, however, that the analysis was originally suggested rather by Aristotle's interest as a biologist in the facts of *organic* development. Suppose we ask, e. g., what was requisite in order that there should now be an oak on this particular spot. We may say (1) there must previously have been a germ from which the oak has grown, and this germ must have had certain actual physical and chemical properties characteristic of the germs from which oaks in particular grow, or there

C.

A Popular Résumé of the main arguments against the Platonic Ideas, with special reference to the "Idea of Good."
   Ethica Nicomachea, 1, 6, 106a 11—b7.

It is perhaps better to examine the notion of a universal good, and to state the difficulties it raises, though such an investigation is distasteful to me, owing to my personal friendship for the inventors of the doctrine of Ideas. Still, it will surely be allowed that it is commendable and even obligatory in defence of truth to abandon even one's own cherished convictions, especially in a philosopher. For

would have been no oak. This is the *material* cause. (2) This germ, though in many respects perhaps not distinguishable from those of other species, must have followed certain special laws in its development; it must have had an initial tendency to grow in the way characteristic of oaks, not that of elms or planes, etc. This is the *form* or formal cause. (3) There must have been an initial movement by which the germ was brought into contact with the external surroundings requisite in order that the process of development may begin — an *efficient* cause. (4) And there must be an ultimate or final stage in the process, a stage in which the germ is no longer developing into something that one day will be an oak, but actually has grown into an adult oak. This is the *end* or *final* cause, in the perfectly literal sense of "end," as the last stage of the process. Aristotle's biological interest leads him to conceive of this final stage of the development as in all cases a conscious or subconscious purpose immanent throughout all the previous stages. (Thus in *organic* development the formal and final causes regularly tend to coalesce in a single conception of an immanent law of growth, which is at the same time a teleological law of a thing's purposive activity.) It will be seen that individual agency is an indispensable element in his notion of causation, and that he has no sense of "cause" exactly corresponding to the familiar modern notion of a mere uniform law of the sequence of *events*. For an excellent brief exposition of the subject, see Siebeck, *Aristoteles* (Frohmann's Classiker der Philosophie, Vol. 8, pp. 32-42).

though both are dear to us, it is a sacred duty to give the preference to truth.[1] Well, the devisers of the theory did not profess to recognize Ideas of aggregates in which there is an order of priority and posteriority (and for this reason they constructed no Idea of the class of numbers). Now, "good" is predicated alike in the categories of Substance, of Quality, and of Relation. But the absolute, i. e., Substance, is logically prior to the Relative (which seems rather to be an accessory or accident of substance), so that there cannot be a common Idea applicable to all these instances.

Again, "good" has as many meanings as "Being." It is predicated in the categories of Substance, e. g., of God or Mind; in that of Quality, e. g., of the virtues; in that of Quantity, e. g., of the due mean; in that of Relation, e. g., of the useful; in that of Time, e. g., of the favourable opportunity; in that of Place, e. g., of favourable climate, etc. So it clearly has no one single, universal sense. If it had, it would not be predicable in all the categories, but only in one.

Again, since the things which fall under a single Idea form the objects of a single science, there ought to be a single science of all "goods" universally. But there are in fact many sciences even of the "goods" which come under a single category. E. g., the favourable opportunity in war is the object of Strategy, in disease of Medicine; the due mean in diet is the object of Medicine, in exercise of Gymnastics.

---

[1] He adroitly excuses his attack by the same apology which Plato had employed for *his* attack on Homer in *Republic*, 595c: "I must speak, said I, and yet I am restrained by the love and admiration I have felt for Homer ever since my childhood. . . . But, after all, a man should not be honoured at the expense of truth; so, as I say, I must speak."

One may also be puzzled even to know what they mean by an "Ideal so-and-so," since it is one and the same definition of man which applies alike to the "Ideal Man" and to an ordinary man. In so far as both are "men," there is no difference between them. Consequently, there is no difference either in the case of "good." Nor, again, will the Idea be any more truly good because it is eternal, just as a thing which lasts a long time is not on that account any whiter than one which only lasts a day.

D.

The alleged Difficulty in the Connection of Mathematics with the Doctrine of Ideas. (Cf. *A*, 9, 992b 12-17.)

Metaphysics, *M*, 2, 1076b 11—39.

Yet, it is not even possible that there should be such separate and independent[1] entities. For if, over and above the solids our senses perceive, there is to be a further set of solids separate from and independent of the former, and logically prior to them, manifestly there must also be separate and independent planes, over and above the planes our senses perceive, and similarly in the case of points and lines; it is all part of the same theory. But, so much being admitted, once again, there must be yet further separate and independent planes, lines, and points, over and above those contained in geometrical solid figures. For isolated entities are logically prior to the same entities in combination; and if

---

[1] κεχωρισμένας, "separated," i. e., existing as distinct objective entities, not merely as products of subjective mental abstraction without a real separate existence of their own. I have employed the double expression "separate and independent" to represent the one Greek word, which it is, however, very tempting to translate simply by "transcendent."

bodies which are not perceptible to the senses are logically prior to bodies which are so perceptible, it follows by the same argument that independent, self-existing planes are logically prior to the planes of the motionless[1] solids. So that these planes and lines are classes distinct from those postulated along with the separate and independent solids. The latter are postulated *with* the mathematical solid figures; the former are logically prior to these figures.

Similarly once more, the planes just referred to will contain lines, and by the same reasoning there must be yet other lines and points prior to these, and besides the points of these "prior" lines there must be yet other points, prior to them, but beyond which there is no further prior class of points. Now, surely, this accumulation of entities becomes an absurdity. For it follows that there is only one class of solids besides those our senses perceive, but three such classes of planes (viz., those which are "beside" the sensible planes, those contained in the mathematical solids, those which are "beside" these), four classes of lines, five of points. Now which of all these are to be the objects of the mathematical sciences? For it will surely not be said that it is the planes, lines, and points which are in the motionless geometrical solid which are the objects of these sciences, since it is always the logically prior classes which are the objects of science.[2]

[1] i. e., purely geometrical, as distinguished from physical "bodies." The difference, according to Aristotle, between the objects of Mathematics and those of Physics is precisely that the former, though "inseparable from matter," are not capable of motion, the latter are "inseparable from matter but not incapable of motion." *Metaphysics, E,* 1026a 18.

[2] The character of the reasoning will become clearer if we consider the simplest of the cases mentioned, that of the plane.

The same argument is applicable also to the case of numbers. For each class of points there will be a different

Aristotle contends that on a realist theory, like that of Plato, which regards the plane surfaces of Geometry not as mere logical abstractions but as objective entities, there must be not only one but three classes of such entities, over and above the perceptible surfaces of physical bodies, viz.: (1) The single archetypal "Idea" of *the* plane, i. e., the entity to which we refer in giving the definition of the plane as such; (2) the entities which figure as constituents in the definition of the geometrical solid, e. g., as determined or bounded by four planes; (3) the infinitely numerous "mathematical planes" which appear in Geometry. It is of these last that "physical" plane surfaces are immediately "copies." Thus he arrives at the following series of entities as all implied in the Platonic theory:

3 classes of plane, viz.: (a) *The* plane as represented by its definition.

(b) The plane as a boundary of solids

(c) "Mathematical" planes.

4 classes of line, viz.: (a) *The* line as represented by its definition.

(b) The line as boundary, or rather as intersection, of planes.

(c) The line as intersection of planes which are boundaries of solids.

(d) "Mathematical" lines.

5 classes of point, viz.: (a) *The* point as represented by its definition.

(b) The point as intersection of lines.

(c) The point as intersection of lines which are intersections of planes.

(d) The point as intersection of lines which are intersections of planes, which are boundaries of solids.

(e) "Mathematical" points.

I must leave the reader to decide whether the ingenuity of all this is not equalled by its perversity, merely observing that "by the same reasoning," there should be *two* and not, as Aristotle says, only *one* class of "solids" over and above "physical" solids.

corresponding class of units,[1] and so again for each class of sensible objects, and again for each class of conceptual objects.[2] Thus the numbers of classes of mathematical numbers will be infinite.

[Aristotle][3] *De Lineis Insecabilibus*, 968a 9—14. (Text of Apelt in the Teubner series.) If there is an "Idea of Line," and the Idea is the archetype of all the objects which fall under the same concept, while the parts of an object are logically prior to the whole which they constitute, the "Ideal Line" must be indivisible. The same will be true of the "Ideal square" and "triangle," and all the other figures, and universally of the "Ideal plane" and "Ideal solid;" for otherwise it would follow that there are things[4] which are logically prior to these entities.

ib. 969a 17-21. Those who construct indivisible lines among the Ideas make an assumption—viz., in postulating Ideas of such objects—which is perhaps of less extended scope than that now under examination,[5] and in

[1] Because a point is simply a "unit having position"

[2] Because each object of sense or thought is a "unit," and also a "copy" of a simple "transcendent" unit.

[3] The author of the essay, though certainly not Aristotle, is almost equally certainly one of his immediate disciples, possibly Theophrastus. See Apelt, *Beiträge zur Geschichte der Griechischen Philosophie*, p. 269.

[4] viz., the lines or planes into which the "Ideal plane," or "solid," if divisible, may, according to the Platonists under discussion, be divided.

[5] The assumption under discussion is that there is a whole infinitely numerous class of indivisible "mathematical" lines, or "infinitesimal" lines, which are, in fact, the entities commonly called *points*. "Aristotle's" objection, as Apelt (*Loc. cit.* p. 274, note 2) explains, is that you cannot infer the indivisibility of "mathematical" lines from the supposed indivisibility of the "Ideal line;" on the

a sense they destroy the force of the very assumptions on which their proof rests. For such arguments are, in fact, subversive of the Ideas.

contrary, the only valid ground for calling the "Ideal line" indivisible would be your previous knowledge that "mathematical" lines, as a class, are indivisibles. You have no right, on Platonic principles, to assume an Idea except when you already know of an existing class of coresponding individual things. There can be no idea corresponding to any class which is inconceivable. Hence, if it can be shown that all "mathematical" lines are divisible, there can be no reason to postulate an "Idea" of the indivisible line.

INDEX OF PROPER NAMES